Exploring Primary Design and Technology

Rob Johnsey

CASSELL

Cassell
Wellington House
125 Strand
London WC2R 0BB

PO Box 605
Herndon
VA 20172

First published in 1998

British Library Cataloguing-in-Publication Data
A catalogue record for this book is available from the British Library.

ISBN   0–304–336181 (hardback)
         0–304–33619X (paperback)

Typeset by The Bill Gregory Partnership, Pevensey, East Sussex
Printed and Bound in Great Britain by: Redwood Books, Trowbridge, Wiltshire

Contents

Dedication

To my father, who taught me much about design and technology.

Part One

Design and Technology in the Primary School

Introduction

There is no doubt that the new curriculum subject Design and Technology is a strange beast. Some will say that it has been lurking in the shadows of the primary curriculum for a long time but in a different guise and with a different name. Others will argue that it has never been seen in this form before and only now is it rearing its fascinating head. To those who have received a largely arts educational background, the subject may have an Art and Design image which in turn might be closely related to the old Art and Craft once found in the primary school. Whereas those with a scientific bias might focus on the word technology and imagine machines, electronics and practical problem solving as the essential elements of the subject.

There is little doubt that the public perception of technology is not the same as that understood by those in education. It is a small wonder, then, that teachers are still in the process of clarifying their own ideas about Design and Technology in schools. Some write of Design and Technology as being two separate subjects while others only imagine the old subject, Craft Design and Technology of the secondary school. Some imagine it to be about making products while others would want it to be about creative thinking skills only.

All the other curriculum areas outlined in the 1988 Education Act have long histories of development often backed-up by extensive research, while Design and Technology in its current form suffers from a dearth of such essential development. Almost all practising teachers as well as student teachers will have studied the other curriculum areas while they were at school and developed a feel for each sphere of study, while this will almost certainly not be so for Design and Technology as we know it today. There is no substitute for spending time in becoming familiar with the vocabulary and rationale for a subject. Some attempts have been made to provide

1

training in Design and Technology for practising teachers and the subject has been a statutory part of all Initial Teacher Training since 1990. These, however, have been made at a time when even the trainers have been coming to terms with an ever changing definition of the subject.

The beast, then, has risen but do we know what we have unleashed? Should the creature be nurtured or stifled, encouraged or ignored? We need to know more about it and what it can do for the education of our children. As with all beasts, Design and Technology has evolved and grown over the past few years but the development has occurred in an uncharacteristically rapid fashion. The subject has changed in nature from what we and its creators all thought it was at its birth. The evolution has been impressive and largely successful but it is still continuing apace. These are exciting times!

Defining Design and Technology for the Primary School

Let us be clear – this subject is no Jekyll and Hyde. Design and Technology is a single curriculum subject with a mind of its own. It possesses a heart and soul that is unique and a strong underlying rationale that is especially suited to the primary school. It is not like science, maths, art or information technology and yet it has strong links with these areas of study and may, indeed, enhance children's learning in all curriculum subjects. It is not solely about design nor entirely about the skills and knowledge of technology. The English language does not have a suitable word to describe the subject so we have to make do with a fudge which may compound our misunderstanding until evolution has moved us all on somewhat.

The Assessment of Performance Unit (APU) set out to explore assessment in design and technology and provides a useful definition for the subject:

> Design and technology . . . 'is an active study involving the purposeful pursuit of a task to some form of resolution that results in improvement (for someone) in the made world. It is a study that is essentially procedural and which uses knowledge and skills as a resource for action . . .'
>
> (Kimbell *et al.*, 1991)

The key ideas in this definition are that Design and Technology is about *improvement* in the made world and therefore cannot proceed without identifying the fact that something requires improvement. This would seem to be a strong justification for teaching the subject to all children, in that it might provide skills and knowledge which would be useful in the future life of the pupil. The idea of improvement, however, needs careful consideration. Different people will have different views about what constitutes 'improvement' and pupils need to be made aware of the kind of value judgements that are made when designing and making. Also the idea of using *knowledge and skills as a resource for action* points to a strong justification for the inclusion of Design and Technology in the curriculum because it can promote learning in other subjects – a theme which is developed later in this book.

Others would argue that technology should involve the use of predominantly scientific knowledge and understanding. Thus Naughton (1994, p. 8) suggests that:

> 'Technology is the application of scientific and other knowledge to practical tasks by organizations that involve people and machines.'

This connection with scientific knowledge appeared in some of the consultation documents preceding the current National Curriculum orders for design and technology:

> 'Technology is the application of scientific and related knowledge to a problem, resulting in a solution which may involve the creation of a product.'
>
> (National Curriculum Council, 1992)

Baynes (1992, pp. 11 and 19) provides a more designerly view of Design and Technology when he suggests:

> 'All design and technology is an attempt to serve human needs, wants and aspirations . . .' and 'Design and technology looks towards the future. Its job is to envisage what should be made. It attempts the difficult task of trying to "see", and then to bring into existence, places, buildings, products and images that society believes it needs.'

The guidance material for design and technology, provided as support for the National Curriculum orders, makes it clear that children with capability in design and technology should be able to 'recognize and explore people's needs and wants, develop ideas about how these might be met and develop products which meet those needs' (SCAA, 1995a, p. 4).

The key features emerging in each of these definitions are that Design and Technology is about:

(i)   responding to the needs of and problems encountered by people;
(ii) developing and making products to suit these needs or solve these problems;
(iii) using designing and making skills together with knowledge and understanding from a broad range of disciplines especially science.

Design and technology can be described as an active response to the needs and problems encountered by people. The response consists of employing:

- procedures and strategies;
- knowledge and understanding;
- practical capability;

to develop and make products, which satisfy the need, or solve the problem.

Design and Technology, then, is not about making 'copy models' by following a set of instructions or a recipe. *Make a model of a Norman hill fort* (using a picture in a book for instance) is not Design and Technology but *Design and make a model of a house of the future which takes into account energy saving devices* could qualify as a suitable task if approached in the right way. A task such as *Write a story to read to a toddler* is not Design and Technology, while *Design and make an apron to protect a toddler as she paints* involves making and evaluating a product and therefore would make a successful project.

A complete design and make task should involve a made product which is produced for a clear purpose (even if the purpose is an artificial one invented by the teacher such as a hat for teddy to use on a sunny day). The skills learnt in making a model hill fort or writing a story might well contribute to those required for Design and Technology but do not provide a complete experience.

Design and Technology and the Primary School Ethos

The primary school is a special place. While each school has its own characteristics and forms of organization there are a number of common elements, some of which will contribute to the successful implementation of Design and Technology. The subject will flourish in the primary school because in most schools, conditions are favourable for its promotion. These conditions include:

A GENERALIST CLASS TEACHER HAS AN OVERVIEW OF THE WHOLE CURRICULUM FOR THE CHILD.

This enables the teacher to identify links between other curriculum areas and Design and Technology. It has already been argued that Design and Technology is about the application of knowledge from other disciplines. The primary teacher is in an ideal position to promote these links thus making Design and Technology a vehicle for learning and reinforcing ideas from other disciplines.

Case study:

A class of pupils were embarking on a cross-curricular topic entitled The Home. The teacher had planned to give them the task of designing and making a model of a folding chair suitable for their own bedroom. The chair could be folded away to provide more space when necessary. The pupils' work in maths had involved them in making measurements accurate to the nearest millimetre and in geography they had looked at the scale of various maps and plans. The teacher saw this as an opportunity to reinforce and apply this work so he asked his pupils to take measurements of the members of the class and scale these down to make a card model 'pupil'. The card model was subsequently used to help in designing the dimensions of the model chairs and in testing the final proportions.

THE CLASS TEACHER IS RESPONSIBLE FOR DELIVERING MUCH OF THE CURRICULUM TO THE SAME CLASS OF CHILDREN.

Design and Technology is often about developing open-ended tasks which give rise to sometimes unexpected links with other subjects. These reinforcing links can be exploited spontaneously by a generalist teacher as they occur in the classroom.

Case Study:

Mrs Brain wanted a group of her children to design and make simple card shadow puppets to tell the story of St George and the Dragon. The children would use the puppet play in an assembly towards the end of term. The children investigated ways of making different shadows, and how to control the movement of some of the puppets by using rods.

As the project continued and the children's interest increased Mrs Brain realized that she could exploit the situation to develop the children's language skills in speaking. She decided to use some of her language time to develop the children's ability to use their voices for special effects. At the same time she adapted what she had planned to do in her music lessons to enable the children to compose sound effects for the play.

PRIMARY SCHOOLS PROMOTE LEARNING THROUGH PRACTICAL WORK

Primary aged children need to learn much through practical experiences. This is often apparent when witnessing the pleasure children get from a practical task. Primary school teachers are already geared up for teaching through practical experiences. Design and Technology merely provides a more meaningful setting for this to happen.

MANY OF THE MATERIALS AND TOOLS REQUIRED FOR PRIMARY DESIGN AND TECHNOLOGY CAN BE MADE AVAILABLE IN THE PRIMARY SCHOOL CLASSROOM

The primary classroom is an extremely flexible workshop in which materials and tools to suit a variety of circumstances can be made readily available. This is particularly useful for a subject such as Design and Technology in which pupils' requirements cannot always be predicted. A well organized teacher will enable the children to collect materials and tools as and when they are required. If the items requested are not available then there is often a suitable alternative to hand.

Case Study:

Jill was making a model Jack-in-a-box using a card container and strips of wood. She wanted to use a flexible spring to mount Jack on so that the toy would leap out when the lid was opened. There were no suitable springs available in the classroom but the teacher was able to talk to Jill about alternatives such as elastic bands or pieces of sponge which were available in a general store. Jill knew just where to find the piece of sponge she needed and went off to search for this while her teacher made a mental note to make a collection of suitable springs for her materials store cupboard.

PRIMARY CLASSROOMS ARE SOMETIMES ARRANGED SO THAT DIFFERENT GROUPS OF CHILDREN ARE ENGAGED ON DIFFERENT TASKS AT ANY ONE TIME

If necessary the teacher is able to arrange for small groups to tackle Design and Technology tasks and to provide these with the special attention which may be required. This may be particularly beneficial when pupils are learning to use more sophisticated materials and tools for the first time.

THE PRIMARY SCHOOL TIMETABLE HAS SOME DEGREE OF FLEXIBILITY

Different curriculum subjects make different demands on school time. A school can arrange its timetable to suit these varying demands. This can be useful for a practical subject which has an open-ended and sometimes unpredictable nature.

THE CROSS-CURRICULAR APPROACH IN MANY PRIMARY SCHOOLS PERMITS REAL CONTEXTS FOR DESIGN AND TECHNOLOGY TO BE EXPLOITED

The educational benefits of cross-curricular studies which are so well championed by the primary school can just as easily be exploited when pupils carry out Design and Technology tasks. Children who do not perceive strict boundaries between subject areas can be encouraged to use knowledge and understanding from other curriculum areas in Design and Technology. Design and Technology can be seen as an umbrella subject in which knowledge and skills from elsewhere can meet and be applied in a meaningful context.

The primary school, then, is potentially an ideal place for the promotion of Design and Technology. This is a distinct advantage that the primary school possesses and should be exploited whenever possible. Parents, governors and the government should be made to appreciate that primary schools can offer experiences that are unique, extremely valuable and may often not be obtained elsewhere in the education system. The development of Design and Technology capability in children, in a supportive and creative atmosphere can be one of the jewels in the primary school crown.

The Nature of Design and Technology

Design and Technology is essentially about carrying out tasks which make improvements in the world by satisfying needs or solving problems. This will involve children in making decisions for themselves when planning and executing their own route through the task. The design and make tasks they undertake will, therefore, be of an open-ended nature and will necessarily have a degree of unpredictability about them. It would be a mistake, however, to believe that there is therefore no teaching to be done. Teachers have a responsibility to intervene appropriately in their pupils' design experiences to enable them to improve their capability, skills and knowledge and understanding in the subject.

The three aspects of Design and Technology that teachers will want to promote in their pupils are:

1 *Understanding the Procedures of Design and Technology*

This involves the identification of the skills that combine to make up how pupils and others design and make products. This understanding also involves knowing when and how to use these skills in different contexts.

2 *Knowledge and Understanding in Design and Technology*

This involves areas of knowledge which are unique to Design and Technology as well as knowledge from other subjects.

3 *Practical Capability*

This involves an understanding of how to handle materials, tools and the related processes. It also involves an ability to solve practical problems. This ability often comes with prolonged involvement with practical tasks such as those associated with many hobbies, DIY or careers involving manual dexterity.

Each of these key areas will be explored in subsequent Parts of this book. The first however, plays such a dominant part in our understanding of Design and Technology that it will be developed further here and in Part two.

Understanding the Procedures of Designing and Making

At the heart of design and technology are the procedures of designing and making. These procedures are what goes on when problems are solved or needs are met – the 'active response' in the definition on page 3. A number of publications describe the procedures as *the design process* or *the practical problem-solving process* and it is often implied that there is only one process which might cover all situations. In understanding the nature of design and technology teachers need to become aware of the things that happen when problems are solved or needs are met successfully. Once teachers have become aware of, and familiar with, these elements of Design and Technology then they can devise ways of promoting successful strategies and assessing children's ability to exercise these.

In this book the term *design process* is used to describe the complete action from when a design and make context is explored through to making and evaluating a product which satisfies an identified need. The *design process skills* describe the separate but overlapping events which, when strung together, make up a whole process. The process skills can be described in terms of the actions made by designers when designing and making. For instance, the process skills of *generating ideas* or *modelling* will be used in different ways at different times while designing and making goes on. Finally, it will often be convenient to use the word *designer* in the text to describe someone who completes the whole process of designing and making.

To begin to answer the question: *What happens when effective designing and making takes place?* we can turn to a variety of publications which purport to describe the design process or the problem solving process. These descriptions either take the form of a theoretical model, often in a flow diagram form, or they are implicit in the text of the publication.

A simplistic linear model for the design and technology process is described by Williams and Jinks (Williams and Jinks, 1985), and is shown as figure 1.1 on the opposite page.

The model suggests that there is a neat set of logical steps to completing a design and technology task. It is typical of many similar examples often adopted by teachers in secondary schools in Craft Design and Technology lessons. A similar example (see figure 1.2 on page 10) was produced by the DES in their booklet Craft Design and Technology from 5–16. (DES, 1987)

This linear description of what might go on during a design and technology task has more detail and is helpful in defining some of the design process skills which might be developed in primary schools today.

Figure 1.1 The Williams and Jinks design Line – (Adapted from Williams and Jinks 1985)

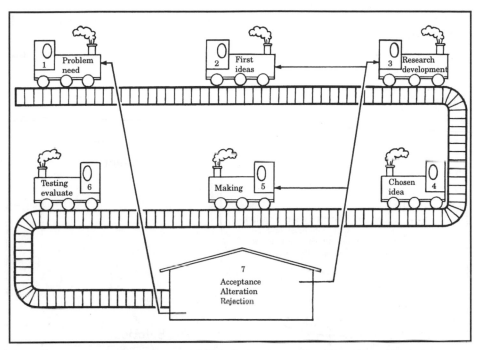

Analysis of a Range of Models for the Design Process

It has been shown that, historically, there has been a surprising consensus of opinion among authors as to the nature of the design process (Johnsey, 1995c). The author has shown that when a range of published models for the process of design are examined, most of them fall into a common pattern in which similar process skills can be identified. These are as follows:

DESIGN PROCESS SKILLS OBTAINED FROM A STUDY OF A WIDE VARIETY OF PUBLICATIONS

- Investigating and exploring the design context.
- Identifying needs, opportunities and potential for design related tasks.
- Clarifying the implications of the design task.
- Specifying criteria for judging the outcome of the design task.
- Carrying out research into the problem and its solution.
- Generating ideas for a product which will provide a solution.

- Modelling ideas – in discussions, as drawings, as mock-ups etc.
- Planning the making of a product.
- Organizing resources.
- Making the product.
- Testing the product.
- Improving the product.
- Evaluating various aspects of the process and the product as work proceeds.
- Evaluating the final product and processes used against original criteria.

Figure 1.2   The DES design loop – (Adapted from DES 1987)

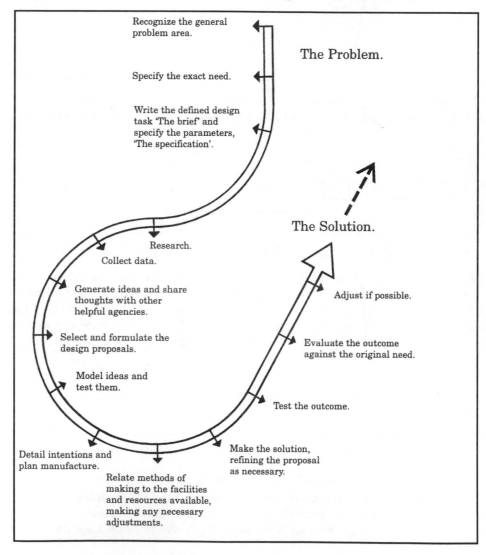

Recognize the general problem area.

The Problem.

Specify the exact need.

Write the defined design task 'The brief' and specify the parameters, 'The specification'.

The Solution.

Research.
Collect data.

Generate ideas and share thoughts with other helpful agencies.

Adjust if possible.

Select and formulate the design proposals.

Evaluate the outcome against the original need.

Model ideas and test them.

Test the outcome.

Detail intentions and plan manufacture.

Make the solution, refining the proposal as necessary.

Relate methods of making to the facilities and resources available, making any necessary adjustments.

The identification, promotion and enhancement of these process skills lies at the heart of Design and Technology teaching and provides the basis for the development of the ideas in this book. Ideas concerning each of these skills are developed in depth in Part 2. At this stage, however, it is worth maintaining a broad overview of designing and making by exploring in detail some more recent models of the design process which have influenced current thinking in the subject.

The Assessment of Performance Unit (APU)

It was through the APU that a radically different view of the process of design emerged. Described as 'the interaction between thought and action' (Kelly *et al.*, 1987) and later as 'the interaction between head and hand' (Kimbell *et al.*, 1991), the model depicts a constant to-ing and fro-ing between thinking and doing.

Figure 1.3   The Assessment of Performance Unit (APU) model (Source Kimbell *et al.*, 1991)

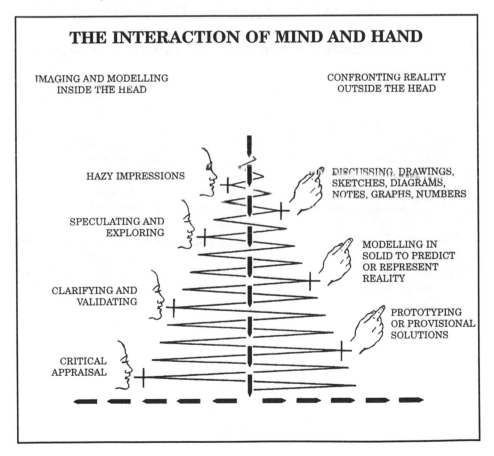

At the beginning of the process one might imagine the introduction of a design problem which immediately leads to some hazy ideas about a solution. This is represented at the top of the model. These hazy ideas will give rise to something being done 'outside the head' such as a comment to a friend, a gesture, a sketch or a prolonged conversation. These actions outside the head will give rise to slightly more refined ideas inside the head. This process of to-ing and fro-ing from thinking to doing is described in the model. The broader base of the model represents a greater development of ideas and action towards solving the problem.

It is a theoretical model which would be almost impossible to observe in reality without knowing what the designer was thinking at all times. It does, however, provide a powerful *view* of what might happen when pupils design and make. It gives us a new image to conjure with, a new standpoint from which to take stock of the design process. It also provides a powerful argument for making assessments of the whole process of designing and making rather than just the parts of it which might be easily recorded in a written paper. This would almost certainly have been a strong motivating factor behind the creation of such a model by a body charged with developing assessment procedures in design and technology.

Observing Primary School Children as they Design and Make

One might suspect that none of the models described so far is based on the direct, systematic observation of pupils as they design and make in a wide range of situations and contexts. Some of the models will be based on previously published ones and may therefore be said to perpetuate a mythical view of what actually happens. Others will be the result of an intuitive and cumulative insight into the way pupils carry out their design and make tasks. Educators, however, are notorious for displaying a need to find tidy models for human behaviour and so it seems reasonable to display a healthy suspicion of such simplistic models.

Theoretical models are all very well but they only describe what others think ought to happen in the classroom. Some current research based on observing children in the classroom as they design and make, suggests that the published models do not necessarily describe what really happens (Johnsey, 1995a).

At this stage it is important to be clear about the type of design process being described. It is possible to identify three types of designer:

1   the professional (expert) designer;
2   the pupil designer;
3   the lay designer.

The professional designer is one who might be considered an expert in the field, having received some form of training. He or she may have specialized in just one part of the whole designing and making process. For instance, many professional designers will pass on the responsibility for manufacture of the product to someone else.

The pupil designer is one who has his or her designing and making behaviour modified by the presence of a teacher or a structured teaching programme.

The lay designer is one who is neither a professional expert nor one who is guided by a teacher or instructor. All human beings become lay designers many times throughout their lives. Pre-school children are a good example. Baynes (1992) points out that young children enter school already able to design and make through their everyday encounters with the world, and goes on to argue that teachers must learn to take this fact into account when devising learning programmes in Design and Technology.

It would seem that the models for the design process that we have explored so far, describe what is hoped will be the behaviour of the pupil designer by emulating the process we believe is used by the professional designer. We know very little, however, about the process of the lay designer when this is applied to primary school pupils. An example of a lay designer might be a primary pupil who carries out a design and make task with a relatively free hand in the classroom. We might begin our understanding of how to enhance pupils' capability in Design and Technology by observing the procedures that they currently use. The following case study is based on classroom research carried out by the author.

Case Study: Lost keys

Ben, a Year 5 pupil, and his partner used a worksheet to make their own set of card keys on a wire ring. The instructions on the worksheet asked them to use any material which was available to design and make a device for recovering the keys from between a crack in two stage blocks. The pair worked well together, making two different devices in the time available. Much time was spent testing the devices and making modifications to these. The first device, a hook on a string, worked well but the second was more problematic.

The teacher's introduction lasted only three minutes. Ben and his partner discussed some ideas briefly using gestures as well as dialogue to model their ideas. The hook and line were quickly produced but more time was spent on testing it than construction. Within a few minutes Ben and his partner were working on another device involving a pair of tongs made with wire. Card 'fingers' were attached to the end of the tongs for improved grip. Some time was spent testing and improving the new device. When the tongs failed to work effectively Ben returned to the first idea and continued to test this. The manipulation of the hook and string tended to require personal skills which needed to be learnt. Eventually Ben returned to the tongs idea and began to adapt this into a scoop. There was not enough time, however, to develop this idea.

A video recording was made of Ben as he carried out his task. This was subsequently analysed by recording the duration of each design process skill displayed by Ben. The behavioural chart for this sequence of actions is shown below.

Figure 1.4 Behavioural chart to show how Ben spent his time during the design and make task. (Source: Johnsey, 1995a)

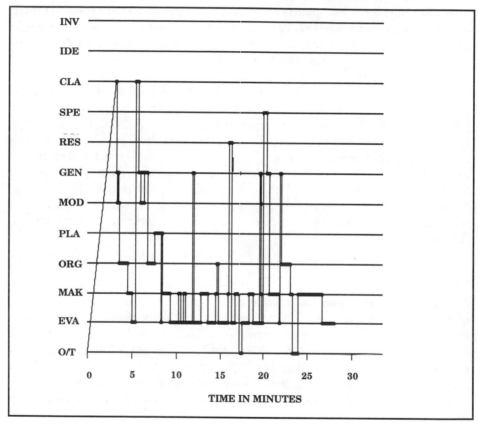

Key:

INV	Investigating	IDE	Identifying
CLA	Clarifying	SPE	Specifying
RES	Researching	GEN	Generating
MOD	Modelling	PLA	Planning
ORG	Organizing	MAK	Making
EVA	Evaluating	O/T	Off task

Each design process skill is shown on the vertical axis and is arranged in the order suggested by a wide range of published linear models for the design process. Time is represented on the horizontal axis so that the whole task can be seen at once. The length of each horizontal bar on the chart, therefore, represents the time for which the behaviour was observed and shows, at a glance, its place, duration and frequency of occurrence in the whole task. The vertical lines are only included to make the graph easier to read and simply demonstrate that one behaviour follows another. The diagonal line at the beginning of the chart represents the time when the teacher is introducing the task and the pupil is sitting listening.

This example comes from a wider study by the author, involving eight case studies of primary school children from reception to Year 5. While it would be inadvisable to generalize too far, it was found possible to construct a typical chart which could suggest how each of the pupils in the study carried out their design and make task

Figure 1.5 A speculative model for the process of design, based on the style of a behavioural chart

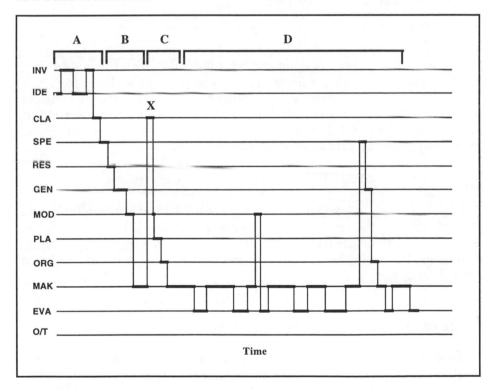

For simplicity and further discussion the whole procedure has been divided into Sections A, B, C and D. In reality there will be no clear boundaries to the behaviours exhibited.

SECTION A

The model shows how the lay designer may begin by investigating a context and, within this activity, begin to identify a situation for which a design and make task is required. At the same time a clarification of what is required will be taking place. This initial part of the design procedure is often provided by the teacher in a school situation. The task setter (i.e. the teacher) will often play a large part in providing specifications for the outcome of the task, although this can be done or added to by the designer /pupil.

SECTION B

In the second stage any combination or sequence of the 'designing' skills (specifying, researching, generating, modelling) might be employed but these lead relatively rapidly to a form of making. This provides experience with the materials and tools which might be used and enables the designer to begin modelling ideas using the materials of construction. Little on-going evaluation will occur here.

SECTION C

Stimulated by the initial making and familiarization with the materials of construction, the designer is likely to return to some of the 'designing' skills as represented by the 'spike' X. This will enable the designer to consider more fully how to go about fulfilling the task by employing researching, generating and modelling skills. This stage may involve more planning and organizing than has previously occurred.

SECTION D

This is a prolonged section, taking up most of the time available and characterized by the *make – evaluate – make* sequences. The nature of the design task will dictate the relative proportions of making and evaluating that occur. There may be instances when the 'designing' skills are revisited for a short period.

General Conclusions from the Study

The generalized model for the design process shown in Figure 1.5 is not the final word on the subject. It is merely another view based on real classroom observation. Furthermore it only provides a window on to what goes on when a pupil is not influenced by the teaching process. It is a beginning, however, and one from which a number of conclusions can be drawn.

The behaviour exhibited in each of the case studies was not the same as that described in published models for the design or problem-solving process. In many instances the behaviours were considerably different, suggesting that a new model, or set of models, is required to describe these particular types of design and make activity.

The activity of making was shown to be dominant in all the case studies. It began early in the activity, before the 'designing' activities were complete, and continued with the same intensity and frequency throughout the whole activity. There is evidence to show that the making activity stimulated and supported all the other design process skills (Johnsey, 1995b).

Many of the designing skills such as specifying, researching and modelling are displayed only for limited periods (and sometimes not at all) and not solely at the beginning of a task. Published models for the design process would suggest otherwise. This may have implications for the way teachers structure design and make activities in the classroom and these are discussed later in Part 2. Children choose to move from one type of design behaviour to another fairly rapidly and there is some evidence to show that the younger they are the more rapid this movement.

The context of the design task and the way the activity is introduced will affect whether certain behaviours are exhibited by the pupil. For instance those behaviours described by many as occurring early on in the design process such as identifying will be absent if the teacher provides a design brief and allows no time for a general investigation. Pupils will often choose to go straight to the heart of a problem rather than carrying out design-related research, especially if there are no obvious resources available with which the research can be carried out.

The Development of Design and Technology Within a National Curriculum Structure

The evolution of a view of the process of design can be charted through the series of documents produced for the National Curriculum firstly in science and later in technology (Johnsey, 1995c). From the first consultative document for science which included technology (DES / WO, 1988) through to Design and Technology in the National Curriculum (SCAA, 1995a) subtle changes in the view of the design process can be charted. In each document the designing and making is not described as a singular process but rather as an implied model. This is achieved through introductory texts, the titles for Attainment Targets and the section headings for Statements of Attainment.

The National Curriculum for Design and Technology (DfE, 1995) clarifies much of this development by employing two sub-headings, Designing Skills and Making Skills where an underlying process of design can be detected which is described with subtle differences at Key Stage 1 and Key Stage 2. In summarizing the requirements for Key Stage 1 and 2, a helpful list of design process skills for the primary school emerges:

Pupils should be taught:

DESIGNING SKILLS:

a)   generate ideas – and use information sources to help in designing (KS2);
b)   clarify ideas;
c)   develop ideas;
d)   model ideas;
e)   suggest how to proceed;
f)   identify strengths and weaknesses (in their design ideas);
g)   indicate ways of improving their ideas – Key Stage 2 only.

MAKING SKILLS:

a)   select materials, tools and techniques;
b)   measure, mark out, cut and shape a range of materials;
c)   assemble, join, and combine materials;
d)   apply finishing techniques;
e)   suggest how to proceed;
f)   evaluate products;
g)   implement improvements – Key Stage 2 only.

These process skills with some modifications will be discussed in detail in the next Part, but first we should explore the helpfulness of the notion of a design process.

The Concept of a Single Process of Design

The overall picture gained from a survey of published literature is convincing in its consistency and possibly reassuring to many primary teachers who need some reliable guidance in a new subject area. If, however, the picture that is painted does not reflect *reality* then the literature may be doing teachers and their pupils a disservice by mis-leading them as to the nature of design and technology. For instance it is easy to find examples of frustrated teachers who complain that the models children make bear very little resemblance to their design drawings. Armed with a clearer view of how children design and make we might ask, first, *Are design drawings always necessary?*, second, *If so what is their function?* and, third, *Should teachers* expect *a close resemblance between the two?*

There are many references in the literature to the use of caution over displaying the design or problem-solving process as a fixed linear or cyclical sequence (DES, 1987; Kimbell *et al.*, 1991; Hennessy and

McCormick, 1994). Baynes (1992, p.1) suggests that, 'The processes involved in designing are *not* linear, they do *not* always start from human needs, and they do *not* always proceed in an orderly way. They *are* reiterative, spiralling back on themselves, proceeding by incremental change and occasional flashes of insight.'

The APU (Kelly *et al.*, 1987) was clear about the disadvantages of making pupils jump through the 'hoops' of a design process. They identified '*Task identification, investigation, generation and development* and *evaluation*' as guiding intentions for pupils with a logical 'evolutionary relationship' but not to be taken as discrete stages in a process.

These 'health warnings' are all very well, but some publications do not provide them and actively set out to give the impression that a particular model is set in stone (Rowlands and Holland, 1989; Williams and Jinks, 1985; Engineering Council/SCSST, 1985). The structure of a single, simplified process imposed on what is an unfamiliar and process-oriented subject may initially be of help to non-specialist primary teachers. It can provide a sense of security and some guidance as to how to proceed. As teachers' perceptions and expertise improve, however, there are dangers in representing pupils' designing activities in such a simplistic way.

An important point to consider here is that the concept of a process presupposes two things. First that it can be identified by the sub-skills involved and represented as a procedural model and second that it can be employed over and over again, possibly in a variety of contexts.

There is evidence to suggest that this may not be the case in design and technology. Hennessy and McCormick (1994) argue that both experts and pupils (who they call novice problem-solvers) use different strategies which are strongly influenced by the context of the design. They go on to suggest that expert problem-solvers' work 'evidently varies with the context in which they are working' and that they use 'considerable knowledge . . . about the problem area'. In contrast, school pupils are 'continually working in unfamiliar contexts' and thereby not holding the expert knowledge necessary for successful designing.

Developing an Understanding of Design and Technology for the Future

Our investigation into the nature of design and technology has taken us to a number of viewpoints in order to gain a clearer picture of the process of design. We have seen that while the process is often described as a tidy, linear set of steps which might be used over and over again in differing situations the reality is often different. There are behavioural character-istics (the design process skills shown on page 9) which can be identified whenever designing and making goes on but the ways in which these are employed will vary and not necessarily fit into a neat pattern which could be taught to pupils. We have explored the characteristics of the way pupils design and make in the primary school with little or no teacher guidance but we do not know yet how the educational process should come to bear on this. Furthermore we do not yet have much idea of how the process employed by a *successful* pupil designer might look. We might be able to recognize a high quality product which is made by a pupil, but we do not yet know how pupils might best arrive at these products.

This section describes a view of design and technology which will enable teachers to plan a coherent learning programme for pupils, which takes account of the current knowledge of the subject.

The Toolbox Model

Teachers must attempt to develop in pupils, a set of skills and strategies which might be used in various appropriate combinations and which are suitable for different design contexts. For instance, we should not assume that it is always appropriate for a pupil to produce a design drawing as a preparation for making a high quality product but, of course, at another time that particular skill might well be useful. Equally, pupils will benefit from knowing about a *range* of evaluative skills (such as scientific testing or the use of a judging panel) and should be able to choose the most appropriate of these strategies to suit the particular context of a design task. The key point here is that any skill or strategy used must be appropriate to the task in hand. Pupils must develop and acquire a collection or 'tool box' of such skills and strategies and know when to use the most appropriate of these.

The 'toolbox' used by effective designers might have a number of layers representing:

1   procedural skills;
2   knowledge and understanding;
3   practical capability.

Each layer can be divided into identifiable sections; Each section will contain a range of 'tools' or strategies.

For instance a section in the procedural skills layer might be labelled *modelling skills*. This section might contain sketching skills, temporarily arranging the materials of construction, making paper mock-ups, using modelling clay, etc.

The toolbox 'image' has a number of features:

- It suggests that these are the things a designer will need to have in order to achieve a purposeful task.
- The 'tools' in the box can be used in any combination and will often be used in conjunction with each other.

- Pupils will need continual practice in using some of the tools and will need experience in using these in different situations.
- The tool collection can be added to in a progressive way.
- New tools can be 'discovered' or 'identified' and put to use at any time.

Figure 1.6   The design and technology toolbox

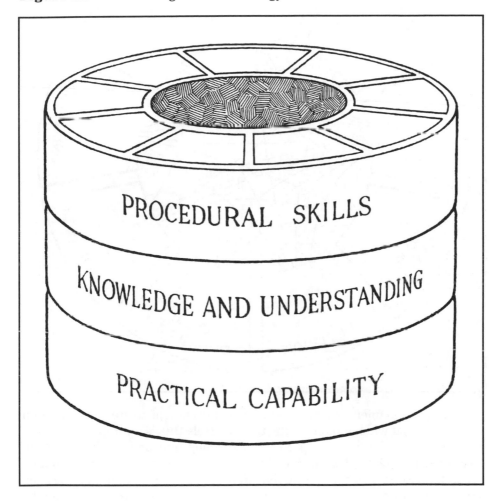

USING THE TOOLBOX IMAGE AS A MODEL FOR THE DESIGN PROCESS

The top layer which holds the design process skills will have a number of compartments each containing a variety of strategies for carrying out a part of the design process. This is illustrated in Figure 1.7 and provides a useful model for describing a broad view of the design process.

Figure 1.7   Toolbox model for the design process

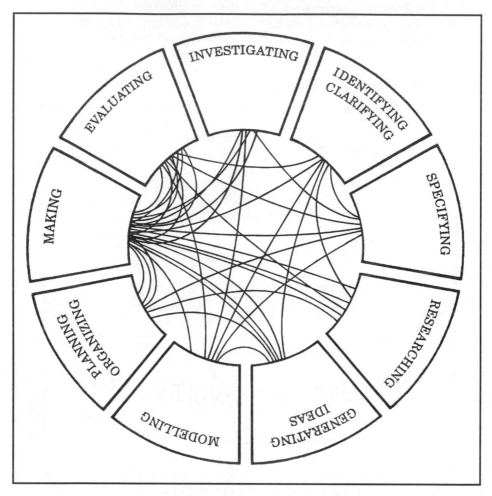

Each compartment can be filled with a collection of strategies which can be drawn upon when a pupil or the teacher feels this is appropriate. One of the teacher's roles is to help children develop and add to this range of strategies in each toolbox section. The toolbox image has a second function. It can be used to suggest *how* pupils might go about designing and making. The curved lines joining the sections represent an imaginary path taken by the designer in completing the design and make task. The lines are arranged to show the following points:

- A designer, tackling a design and make task, might begin anywhere in the toolbox.
- The designer may choose to move from one design process skill to any other. There is no suggestion that there is a fixed linear route.

This route will be different when working within different contexts.

- The same process skill will be revisited a number of times, some more than others.
- There is no suggestion that 'designing' skills should precede 'making' skills. The model shows how these dovetail into each other.
- The effective designer will choose the most appropriate route from section to section and between each toolbox layer.
- The effective designer will choose the most appropriate tool or strategy while visiting each section.
- The importance of *making* for the primary-aged pupil is shown by more lines going to and coming from this section. There is evidence to show that making is a stimulus to and a vehicle for many of the other process skills. (Johnsey, 1995b)
- The inter-relationship between making and evaluating is illustrated by a predominance of connecting lines.

Creativity in Design and Technology

The toolbox model should not be seen as a mechanistic way of describing design and technology. It provides an analysis of the separate skills and understanding involved but should not suggest that these are used without regard to the wider task. If being creative is about combining a variety of elements into something which has not been made before, then the toolbox suggests how the creative pupil might be encouraged to do this. It is the choice of tools, the route taken from one to another and the way in which the tools are used in combination that will distinguish one designer from another.

A question which has yet to be addressed is 'How do teachers teach pupils to become better and better at choosing the route they take through a design and technology task?'

The next Part will explore the tools or strategies which might be found in each section of this layer of the toolbox. It will discuss ways in which teachers can encourage their pupils to gain these tools and how the pupils might be taught how to choose the best one for each occasion. Subsequent Parts of this book will explore the other layers of the toolbox – knowledge and understanding and practical capability.

Part Two

Developing Designing and Making Skills

Introduction

'Children with design and technology capability are able to recognize and explore people's needs and wants, develop ideas about how these might be met and develop products that meet those needs.'

(SCAA 1995b, p 4)

Effective designing and making is about selecting from an ever widening repertoire of process skills and combining these with an increasing knowledge and understanding. The process skills were identified in Part 1 and will be explored in more detail now. Children will use these skills in various combinations to achieve their designed products. In deciding which to use and when, in a particular context, they will be developing their overall capability. Teachers will need to be familiar with the various 'tools' which could be placed in the toolbox and will want to put emphasis on certain ones within any particular learning experience.

1: Investigating Contexts, Identifying Needs and Specifying Outcomes

Investigating a Context for Designing and Making

Pupils involved in investigating a context for designing and making will be exploring and evaluating a broad area in which artefacts, systems or environments are found. They may or may not be aware of the design task they will be involved in. They will be gathering information on, and gaining experience with, a wide range of situations which might be related to the design task they will carry out. An example of this skill might be listening to a story in which there is potential for meeting needs or solving problems, or going on a trip out of school to a local supermarket which might set the scene for a variety of design and make tasks to be explored later.

The skills the children develop at this stage are largely investigative and may occur as a result of work in another curriculum area. For instance children studying the life style of the Romans in history might be investigating a context in which water has to be transported across a valley in an aqueduct. This context may well be the starting point for a design and make activity in which a similar problem is dealt with. In religious education a study of festivals may provide the context for designing and making a suitable dish for a celebration. In some instances the teacher will rely upon the children's previous knowledge and experience of a context rather than providing further experiences in this investigative stage. However, we might expect that the more children know about the broad area within which they will be working, the richer will be their design and make experience.

Appropriate background information for a design and make task can be gained by children in a variety of ways. They might carry out a survey of the school playground and compare this with other play spaces. They may be involved in interviewing people to gain an insight into how they view the world on certain issues. An exploration of kitchen utensils used by their grandparents might involve observational sketches, sorting and classifying and testing the effectiveness of mechanisms. Measurements of the human body, made in a maths lesson, might provide the starting point for a consideration of clothing needs in a design and make assignment. Skills such as recording information, analysing data and drawing conclusions based on evidence will all be used in a broad investigation into a suitable context for design and making.

The following is a list of general broad starting points or contexts for design and make assignments:

Clothing:
Exhibitions:
Festivals:
Furniture:
Historical contexts:
      Invaders and settlers;
      Life in Tudor times;
      Local history;
      etc;
Leisure and recreation:
Parties and celebrations:
Pet care:
Playgrounds:
Puppets:
Shops and shopping:
The circus/fairground:
The classroom:
The community:
The garden:
The home:
The picnic:
The school:
The weather:
Toys:
Transport and communications:
Contexts found within stories e.g.:
      The three little pigs;
      The lighthouse keeper's lunch;
      The iron man.

Toolbox skills – Investigating a context

Children should develop an ability to:

- gain an overview of a context;
- listen to and understand information;
- see things from the viewpoint of others;
- carry out general surveys using lists and/or maps or plans;
- observe closely;
- make measurements;
- interview others to gain significant information;
- carry out scientific tests and investigations;
- record information;
- analyse information;
- draw conclusions;
- evaluate others' designed products.

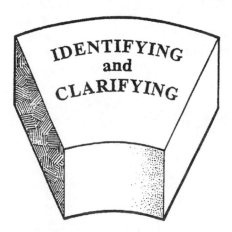

Identifying Needs and Opportunities and Clarifying the Design and Make Task

A design and make activity may develop as the result of a difficulty which must be overcome such as the need to reach things from a high shelf; an improvement which could be made, i.e. redesign the classroom furniture, or as an addition to what already exists (developing a new computer game).

Pupils identifying needs and opportunities will be observing and exploring a context in which design tasks might arise. At the same time they will be actively involved in suggesting problems which might be solved, needs which might be met or opportunities for designing and making. They may identify a client or a set of clients as recipients for the designed product(s) and show an awareness of their needs.

One way to help pupils towards identifying their own design and make tasks is to provide them with a wealth of experience in fulfilling tasks set by others. When they move on to identifying their own tasks, however, they might consider the potential client for the designed products and the various locations in which this client operates. For instance pupils might consider the problems and needs that arise for themselves and their friends in different locations such as their bedroom, their homes, their route to school, the school playground, the classroom etc. They might also be encouraged to consider different times of the day. What particular problems arise first thing in the morning? And so on.

Considering Different Clients

A consideration of fictional characters from a story or a television series provides a good starting point for many design and make tasks. Not only can the story provide the client but it can also provide the problem or need to be satisfied. Pupils will benefit from working within the constraints of a short story when they are expected to identify design opportunities of their own.

Pupils can consider people familiar to them and problems they might have, e.g. parents or pupils younger than themselves. They might go on to consider those less fortunate than themselves and their particular problems, e.g. those confined to a wheelchair. An ideal introduction to considering the needs of others would be for the pupils to have the chance to listen to a visitor to the school and perhaps be able to ask questions about their day-to-day lives.

When considering the needs of others who are inaccessible to the pupils the use of role play may be of benefit. Pupils who are able to imagine themselves in the place of others are in a much better position to consider their needs and problems.

Evaluating the Designed Products of Others

Products which have been designed and made by others can be used by pupils to appreciate the problems the products were designed to solve. For example pupils who are able to look at and handle a collection of writing implements such as a quill pen, a fountain pen and a ball point pen can be encouraged to identify the specific problem which each pen overcomes. The link between the designed product and the initial need or problem is an important one which will be explored in more depth later in this Part. The following is an example of a guide sheet to evaluating products which emphasizes this link.

Figure 2.1   Guide sheet for pupils

HOW WERE PROBLEMS SOLVED IN THE PAST?

Name of object: _____
What does the object do?
Make a sketch.

On your sketch label the materials used to make the object and any parts which have a particular name.

Think of the person who designed the object.
•   What sort of person do you think the designer made the object for?

•   What do you think was used before the object was invented?

Here is a BACKWARDS CARTOON for a ball point pen. It shows what people used before each new invention.

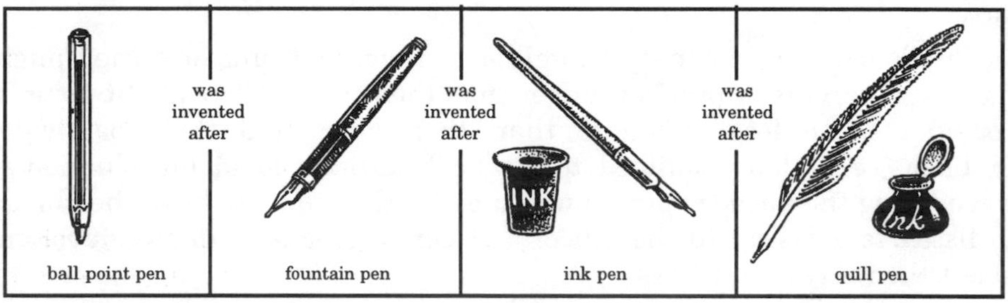

| ball point pen | was invented after | fountain pen | was invented after | ink pen | was invented after | quill pen |

The ball point pen overcame the problem of carrying runny ink and leaks.
Draw a BACKWARDS CARTOON for your object

Which problems were overcome when your object was invented?

Suitable objects which can be evaluated by pupils using the guide sheet opposite:

- penknife;
- electric egg whisk;
- torch;
- Pritt Stick.

Open and Closed Design and Make Tasks

All design and make tasks can be placed on a continuum where at one extreme there are very open-ended tasks involving many choices and decisions to be made by the pupil. At the other extreme closed tasks might be set in which there are very few choices to be made.

Figure 2.2 Closed and open-ended tasks: a continuum

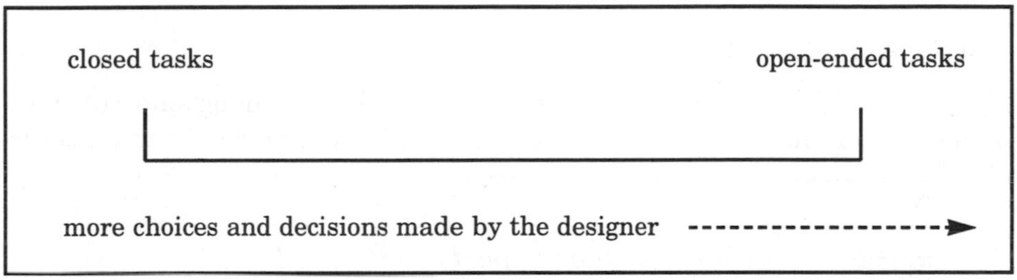

closed tasks   open-ended tasks

more choices and decisions made by the designer - - - - - - - - - - - - - - - - ▶

Pupils in the primary school should experience a wide range of types of task from open to closed ones. However, while pupils are gaining experience in design and technology we might expect them to progress generally from having few decisions and choices towards having more.

Pupils can be given decisions to make about the following broad areas of a design and make task:

Which materials can be used in construction?

A model shopping bag made from sugar paper is less of a challenge than one made from a wider range of materials.

Who the product is for?

A pupil who is told that the greetings card she is about to make is for a grandparent will not need to make decisions about who to send it to.

The number of purposes for the product

A pupil asked to make an article of clothing which protects the wearer from splashed paint will have less to think about than if it was to protect from the general wear and tear of the reception classroom.

The scale of the product

Pupils will have less to think about if they are told the scale to which they should be working. This can often be achieved by providing materials of a particular dimension such as small cardboard boxes from which a model house might be made.

The method of construction

A pupil who is told to use glue to join the fabric finger puppet will have less of a challenge than one who has a free choice as to how this might be done.

The finish applied to the product

A task in which it is more important that a vehicle rolls along smoothly will be less demanding than one in which the final appearance of the model is also important.

The number and scope of functioning parts on the product

In some cases teachers can suggest that only part of a model is redesigned, leaving other, more complicated parts as a simple mock-up.

Case Study – Supermarket Trolley

Some children were working on a design for an improved supermarket trolley. Their teacher had asked them to ignore the problem of the swivelling wheels on the trolley and to concentrate on the problem of the basket design. The children made decisions about the need to separate the fruit and vegetables from the other purchases and about the overall appearance of the trolley. They fitted a baby seat and made toys for it to play with during the shopping. To complete their model, they glued on simple card wheels which did not turn, feeling quite satisfied with having solved a number of other problems concerning the use of the trolley.

If any of the decisions outlined above are made by the teacher the task becomes more closed. This may allow the pupil to concentrate on significant aspects of the task rather than be overwhelmed by its complexity. The following example illustrates how a similar task can be made progressively more open by using a slightly different form of words each time.

From Closed to Open-ended Tasks

MAKING DESK TIDIES

1   Make the model of a pencil holder. Follow the instructions carefully. (Diagram included.) Decorate the pencil holder with felt pens;
2   Use the sheet of A4 card and glue to make a pencil holder for your desk;
3   Choose your own materials to make a pencil holder for your desk;
4   Make something to prevent your pencil rolling off the desk;
5   Solve this problem: Writing equipment often falls off a desk;
6   Explore the problems involved in organizing the equipment on your desk.

Clarifying the Design and Make Task

In many instances in the primary classroom the design and make task will be identified and chosen by the class teacher. This enables suitable tasks to be chosen which:

(i)   are appropriate to the children's interests and abilities;
(ii)   involve skills and understanding which the teacher wants the children to learn;
(iii) involve materials and tools which are available in the classroom;
(iv)   enable links with other curriculum areas to be made.

When the design task is set by the teacher there will be a period when clarification is sought by the pupil or group of pupils. Clarification will probably precede the generation of solutions to the problem but may well be intermingled with this stage. The following features may need to be clarified regarding the design task:

- What exactly does the problem setter require?
- What is the intended purpose for the outcome?
- Who is the outcome for?
- What is the scale of the outcome?
- What materials are available?
- What time and space are available?
- Should the outcome be a model or the real thing?

Clarification of the task will evolve as the designing and making proceeds and may never be complete, even at the end of the task.

Toolbox Skills – Identifying and Clarifying

Children should develop an ability to:

- identify the needs of different clients for a design and make task;
- carry out role play in order to identify with the needs of others;
- evaluate the designed products of others;
- change an open-ended task into a more closed one when appropriate;
- ask clarifying questions about the design brief they have adopted.

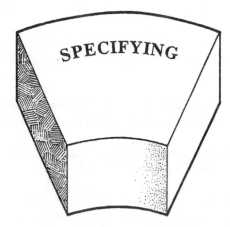

Specifying the Requirements and Purpose of the Outcome

Pupils who are specifying the requirements of the task outcome will be creating the criteria by which they or others might judge how well they have done. The specification will be a statement, spoken or otherwise, of the objectives for the task. Various specifications for the task may be added or subtracted as work proceeds and will often only reside in the mind of the designer and perhaps be taken for granted. For instance a pupil making a greetings card for his grandmother may be able to specify that it should have a moving, pop-up part but take it for granted that the card should stand upright on a horizontal surface. During construction, specifications such as 'The card should be safe to handle' may emerge in the light of experiencing a paper fastener with a sharp edge.

Specifying what should be achieved in a design and make task is closely related to the way it is evaluated at all stages during its construction. If a clear purpose is established for a designed product then evaluation involves establishing whether that purpose has been achieved or not.

Case Study: – Picnic Boxes

A Year 2 class of children were exploring a topic called Summertime. Part of their work involved planning for a picnic by designing and making model picnic boxes to carry food and drinks. The model boxes would be made out of card and reinforced with small strips of wood but there were many realistic features which could be achieved within this simple construction.

The children were encouraged to talk about the essential features they wanted their boxes to have. Some suggested compartments to separate the sandwiches, fruit and drink. They all agreed that the box should have a handle and a catch to keep the lid shut. The teacher suggested that the box be made full size and be made stronger by the addition of short wood strips glued to the corners. A short list of specifications was drawn up on a large sheet of poster paper and displayed in the classroom. As the children worked over a period of weeks they were able to refer to this list and remind themselves of what they were trying to achieve. At the same time they added their own specifications, often without thinking consciously about this. Some decided to decorate their box with tissue flowers while others glued small feet on their box to keep it off the ground.

When it came to evaluating the final product the lists of specifications was used to help discuss each aspect of the model, thus providing a more in-depth judgement as to the success of each product.

Often a teacher in setting a design and make task will provide a set of specifications for the final product.

Design and make a game which can be played on a table top. Your game should be built in the lid of a card box and involve a marble. Make your game suitable for a friend in your class.

At other times the design task could leave the choice of specifications to the pupil.

Design and make a toy with a moving part.

The specifications for this task which could be developed by the pupil might be:

- The toy should be suitable for a four year old.
- It should be made from a durable material such as wood or plastic.
- It should be safe to play with.
- It should teach the child something about the alphabet.

Other specifications could be added as the task proceeds. Children might be encouraged to record the new specifications or these might remain as spontaneous thoughts in the head.

The essential question to ask the pupil is 'What do you want your designed product to achieve? How will you know how well you have done when you have finished?' All design and technology products should be made for a purpose. Creating a list of specifications is one way of defining that purpose more clearly. Once a clear purpose has been established then evaluation becomes more meaningful and profound.

Examples of design and make tasks and the specifications which might be associated with them are:

Design and make a model of a climbing frame for a school playground.

Specifications

- The frame should be suitable for four to seven year olds.
- It should include a slide.
- It should have a protective surface underneath.
- The model should be strong enough to hold a kilogram mass.

Design and make a new container to hold Smarties

Specifications

- The container should hold about 50 Smarties.
- A lid should stop the Smarties falling out even when it is upside down.
- The container should look attractive to a child.

Strategies to Encourage Pupils to Make Specifications for Their Products

Teacher–pupil discussions

All designed products have a list of specifications associated with them. Pupils need to recognize this fact through discussion initially and later by recording in a more formal sense. Thoughtful questioning by the teacher will often help a pupil clarify the specifications she is working to.

Limit the number of specifications considered at any one time

The list of specifications for a product could often be endless. There is no need to define all the specifications for any one product, a focus on three or four of these often being sufficient.

Be aware of the range of different types of specification

The following are the different types of specification which might be considered by primary school children:

Specifications regarding:
- the client – who is the product for? Is there an age range?
- the materials used for construction – is there a limit to the materials available?
- the method of construction – e.g. which methods of joining are available?
- the strength of the product – which parts of the model should be strong and in what way?
- the scale of the product – is it full size or scaled down?
- the appearance of the product – is this to be considered or not?
- the safety of the product – is it safe for all those using it?
- the function of the product – does it do what it is supposed to do?
- the reliability of the product – does it work every time?
- the human and environmental impact of the product.

Teachers would want to place emphasis on a small number of these categories of specification at any one time.

Understanding the Specification Others have made for Design Products

When pupils explore products which have been designed by others they can consider the specifications the designer might have been working to. For instance they might examine a collection of hats from straw sun hats to motorcycle crash helmets. For each hat children can be asked what was the designer trying to achieve in designing the hat in this way? For a sou'wester the specification might have been to keep as much rain water off the wearer as possible as well as producing a hat which was durable and easily stored in a pocket. A fashionable wedding hat will have a quite different function and set of specifications.

Pupils might be encouraged to draw up specifications for their designed products by using a guide sheet similar to the one illustrated in Figure 2.3.

Children might need to be introduced to the term *product* as the thing they are going to make and the teacher might want to focus attention on a limited number of types of specification suggested on the guide sheet. The 'person' for whom the product will be made could of course be the pupil or even a fictional character like a teddy bear from a story.

Figure 2.3 Pupil guide sheet for specifying the outcome of a design and make task

---

SPECIFICATIONS FOR A DESIGN AND MAKE TASK

My design and make task is

The 'person' who will use what I make is

My specifications for my product
Write down the things you want your product to achieve by thinking of some of these ideas.

SAFETY	APPEARANCE	STRENGTH
DOES IT WORK?	RELIABILITY	FUN
MATERIALS	SIZE	

1. I want my product to

2. I want my product to

3. I want my product to

4. I want my product to

Broad or Focused Specifications

Pupils may need help in phrasing their specifications in progressively more useful ways. A specification such as *I want my model playground swing to be strong* is written in fairly vague terms and will not be of great use when making judgements about the product during an evaluation. A statement like *I want my model swing to be strong enough to hold a Plasticine model person that I have made* is much more specific and therefore helpful when an evaluation is carried out.

Sometimes a pupil will find it difficult to be very specific at the beginning of a design task but may find it possible to refine the specification as the task proceeds. For instance a child who begins to design and make a balloon powered vehicle may specify initially that it should simply move along the table. As the model evolves, however, this specification might be made more demanding by adding that the vehicle should move at least 2 metres in a straight line.

The following are some common specifications written in vague terms with examples of how they could be made more meaningful. In most cases simple questioning by the teacher can help children change a broad specification into a more specific one.

Broad specification	More specific requirement
I want my toy to be safe.	I want my toy to have no sharp edges and have no parts which could come loose and be swallowed by a four year old.
I want my new cereal to taste nice.	I want my new cereal to appeal to more than half the children in my taste survey.
I want my model paper bag to be strong.	I want my model paper bag to have handles which withstand a pull of ten Newtons.
I want my model shopping centre to have plenty of parking spaces.	I want my model shopping centre to have parking spaces for 15 cars at a time which is within easy walking distance of the shops.

The purpose for which a product is designed and made in the primary classroom is often only partly appreciated by pupils and teachers alike. The recording of specifications for the product is one way to help clarification on this matter. Without this clarification as to the purpose and hoped for achievement in the product there can be very little meaningful evaluation. This essential relationship between purpose, desired achievement and evaluation of the product is examined further in the next section.

Toolbox skills – Specifying

Children should develop an ability to:

- consider the needs of the potential user of the product;
- rephrase vague intentions for a product into progressively more specific ones;
- add specifications for a product as designing and making proceed;
- be aware of different types of specification they could make for their products.

2: Evaluating Products and Procedures in Design and Technology

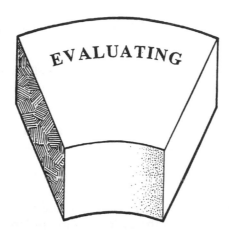

Introduction

The skill of evaluating is a broad and complex one which is employed in a wide variety of situations in the primary school curriculum. In design and technology it is helpful to consider four types of evaluating:

- Evaluating the pupil's completed product and the procedures used to make it – *end-on evaluation*.
- Evaluating the pupil's partially completed design proposal or model – *on-going evaluation*.
- Evaluating the pupil's procedures while designing and making – *procedural evaluation*.
- Evaluating the designed products of others.

Pupils will benefit from the evaluation of others' designed products in a number of different ways. The contribution such work makes to *Identifying needs and opportunities* and *Specifying the requirements and purpose of the outcome* have already been discussed. The skills involved will also be employed when pupils carry out *Research to support designing and making* and this is discussed at length in section 3.

Evaluating the Pupil's Work in Design and Technology

Pupils will be evaluating when they make assessments and checks and/or carry out tests on their work and their procedures during the task and when it is finished. The evaluation may be subjective or objective or a combination of both. They may ask the opinion of others or rely solely on their own judgement. Evaluation can often be identified by the teacher by observing the action which results from it. For instance a simple (unobservable) evaluative thought process may result in an observable modification of the product.

Evaluation may be in the form of a fleeting thought process with no apparent action taken or, at the other extreme, a long-term testing procedure resulting in clearly recorded data which is subsequently analysed and acted upon. It may include the minute by minute assessments made throughout a design task as well as the more considered retrospective assessment made as part of the end of the task.

The Link With the Purpose and Specification for the Product

Evaluations are best made against well defined criteria rather than in a vague generalistic way. Asking a child 'What do you think of your model?' or 'Do you like your model?' is fairly pointless and will almost always exact the same kind of answer from the child. A more in-depth evaluation can be made by taking a number of criteria by which the product might be judged and devising effective ways of determining whether these have been achieved. These criteria are the same as the specifications the pupil will have mapped out earlier on in the design process. A well devised criterion will make the evaluation procedure relatively simple. For example the specification that the hat should fit snugly on the Teddy's head leads to a simple evaluative test to see if it does. If a child specifies that the swing must hold the weight of a Plasticine person, then the evaluative test involves placing the model person on the swing seat and observing what happens. A pupil who states: 'I want my new cereal to appeal to more than half the children in my taste survey', has already committed himself to a particular form of evaluation and a standard against which he can measure how successful he has been.

Objective and Subjective Evaluation of Designed Products

Evaluation of the products of design and make tasks can be made subjectively or objectively depending on the type of criteria being judged. A specification which states that a product should be attractive in appearance will lead to a subjective evaluation being made either by the designer alone or through a wider opinion survey. If a shopping bag is being designed to carry a certain volume of shopping (for instance the equivalent of ten toilet rolls) then the test for this will be an objective measurement of the bag's capacity in standard or non-standard units of volume. Some criteria against which the effectiveness of a product can be judged lead to either subjective *or* objective testing. A specification that the handles on a model shopping bag should be comfortable could be tested in two ways. In one instance individual judges could hold the loaded bag and give their opinions as to the comfort level. An objective test, however, might involve monitoring the pressure exerted by the bag handles by measuring how deeply they cut into a lump of Plasticine.

Carrying Out Objective Evaluations

Objective tests on completed or partially completed designed products will involve some kind of measurement and may well involve a science investigation or experiment. The experiment may not take long (a few minutes) but will involve many of the skills promoted within the maths and science curriculum.

Case Study – Model Boat

John and Susan were making a model boat which was to be propelled by a paddle driven by an elastic band. During construction of their model they spent some time trying out different combinations of elastic bands to see which was the most effective. They found that some bands were too short and others seemed too thin. They soon discovered that three thin bands together worked the best.

Once they had finished their boat they wanted to measure its performance by timing it over a given distance as it moved across the school pond. They made a number of trials and took the average time over 2 metres. They were then able to measure how far it would travel for a certain number of winds of the paddle. They finally wrote a report for the rest of the class based on their findings.

The science investigations involving the elastic bands were carried out informally and quite quickly. Predictions were made, observations carried out and conclusions drawn all within a few minutes. The evaluation involved an objective comparison of different kinds of elastic band.

A more formal and lengthy experiment was embarked upon when the pupils measured the performance of their completed paddle boat. This took longer and was well planned. Measurements were taken and recorded and a written report was produced. Susan was able to suggest that the shape of the boat hull could be improved to avoid creating so much disturbance in the water. This was the result of her close observations and some previous knowledge about boats and how they move efficiently through the water.

This case study illustrates the potential for science investigations to support the process of evaluation in design and technology both during designing and making and as a part of the end-on evaluation.

Other objective tests can be carried out on the products of design and technology by measuring in various ways as the following table illustrates.

Figure 2.4   Table to show examples of how the results of objective tests can be measured

Objective test	Measured with	Measured in	Example
The load on a structure	Non-standard units such as marbles or toy cars Force meter Masses	Marbles or Newtons	Place masses on a bridge until it collapses
The time a vehicle takes to go a given distance	Egg timer Stopwatch	Seconds Minutes	Time a balloon powered vehicle across the classroom
The capacity of a container such as a bag or truck	Lego bricks Centimetre cubes Water	Number of 'bricks' Millilitres of water	Make a shopping bag to hold five litres
Area of material or space used	By direct comparison Squares	Rank order Square centimetres etc	Make a glove puppet using a limited area of fabric
The number of times a device performs correctly	Count number of trials	Number	Testing the reliability of a pop-up card to perform consistently
The temperature of a pot of tea	Thermometer Datalogging equipment	Arbitrary units Degrees Celsius	Design and make a tea cosy
The distance a toy boat moves	Non-standard units such as drinking straws Metre tape	Straws Centimetres Etc	Test an elastic band powered boat for ten winds

Carrying out Subjective Evaluations

Subjective evaluation is no less scientific than the objective kind but depends largely on opinion rather than hard measurement. The effects of biased opinion can be partially overcome by asking more than one opinion and by employing impartial observers. This may be easier said than done in the primary classroom but the principles could be discussed.

Case Study – Playground Apparatus

A group of six year old children were thinking about their school playground and the lack of things to play on. They were challenged by their teacher to use a construction kit to make models of the things they would like to see in the playground. They made a variety of models such as a swing, a see-saw and a simple roundabout. They were very much constrained by the construction kit they were using and the components available, but they learnt a great deal about simple mechanisms with the help of their teacher.

The teacher decided to develop the children's sense of evaluation by helping them to organize a panel of judges made up of their friends in the classroom. The children made up a short list of three things by which their models could be judged:

- *Does the model playground apparatus look good?*
- *Would each model be safe to play on?*
- *Would the model be fun to play on?*

In a reporting session the designers described why and how they had made their models and were followed by the 'judges' who reported their views to the whole class.

Quite often subjective evaluation will be made by the designer alone but as pupils progress they can be encouraged to justify their opinions and to become more critical about their work.

Strategies for Encouraging Children to Evaluate Subjectively

Strategies for encouraging *subjective* evaluation include:

- Establish a set of criteria against which judgements might be made.
- Encourage pupils to tackle one criterion at a time when making their judgements.
- Use the idea of giving marks out of 10 or 100 for different aspects of a product. The marks given by a set of 'judges' can be added up to give an overall mark.

- Encourage pupils to set up consumer tests in which variables (such as quantity to be tasted in a taste survey) are controlled, thus making a test as fair as possible.
- As pupils progress avoid vague criteria such as 'The product must look good'. Be more specific by stating which aspect must look good, what looking good actually means and state to whom should it appeal.
- Discuss with pupils how opinions can be biased and how a representative sample should be used in a survey. For instance it would be wrong to ask only a group of 11 year olds what they felt about a cereal designed and produced for a wider range of ages.
- Provide evaluation sheets with focused questions relevant to the product to guide pupils.

The following table illustrates the link between the specification for a product and the method of evaluation required to test if it has been achieved. It also illustrates how certain types of criteria lead to objective or subjective evaluations. The examples are based on the Supermarket as a context for design and make tasks.

Figure 2.5 Table to show the relationship between design criteria and methods of evaluation (Source: Johnsey, 1995a)

Product	Criterion The product should:	Subjective methods of evaluation
Supermarket trolley	. . . separate fruit and vegetables from rest of shopping	Success/failure judged by potential users of the trolley
A new cereal	. . . look good	Judging panel gives score out of ten for each sample
Display stand for sweets	. . . attract children	Observing stand being used in the shop
Supermarket shopping bag	. . . have comfortable handles	Ask a group of consumers to test subjectively and give opinions

Product	Criterion The product should:	Objective methods of evaluation
Supermarket trolley	. . . hold 500 cubic centimetres (scaled down week's shopping)	Find out how many centimetre cubes the trolley will hold.
Design a new cereal	. . . not contain any added sugar	Yes/No.
Display stand for sweets	. . . allow sweets to flow smoothly into bags	Test operation a number of times for reliability.
Supermarket shopping bag	. . . have comfortable handles	Measure the amount the handle of a loaded bag presses into a lump of Plasticine.

On-going Evaluation

On-going evaluation involves the minute-by-minute judgements and decisions made by the designer. Evidence suggest that this is closely related to the dominant theme of making in primary design and technology (Johnsey, 1995a). It largely consists of regular checks on the suitability of materials and the partially completed product. Someone preparing a food product will often taste a little of the partially completed dish and a pupil making a full sized pair of card Roman sandals will need to make numerous fittings as progress continues.

Strategies for Encouraging Children to Make On-Going Evaluations

Pupils can be encouraged to make on-going evaluations in the following ways:

- Appropriate teacher intervention. Often a sensitive but searching question from a teacher will lead to a pupil making a check on the product in hand.

Answer these questions as you make your card

(1) Is your card a rectangle to begin with?
(2) Does your card fold neatly down the centre?
(3) Will the person the card is for like the picture you have planned for your card?
(4) Does the moving part work smoothly in the mock-up you made?

- Use of a planning sheet which suggests a series of on-going checks to the model as it is made. For instance the planning sheet for a folding greetings card might include the questions on page 47.
- Pupils of all ages will benefit by being asked to pause at appropriate moments during their designing and making to reflect on the progress they are making. Some children tend to want to finish their work quickly and with very little thought as they proceed. A teacher can intervene and ask a group or the whole class to spend a few minutes considering such questions as:

---

(1) Have you chosen the best materials for the job – are there some more appropriate ones?

(2) In the light of your experience so far are there any parts of your design proposal you might want to change?

(3) Are some things working out better than you had expected? If so why is this?

Pupils sharing the experiences and ideas of others for short periods during a shared design task can benefit a great deal.

Evaluating Procedures

So far the evaluation of products or partially finished products has been discussed. Primary school pupils can also be expected to make evaluations of the way in which they arrived at a product. Their design and make procedures can be evaluated while they are working and when they have finished by considering questions such as the following:

ON-GOING EVALUATION OF PROCEDURES

- Do you know the purpose of the product you are making?
- Is there any information you could find out to help you design and make the product?
- Have you tried out some ideas for your product by thinking or drawing or discussing with a friend?
- Have you organized the space in which you will work in the best way?
- Do you have all the tools and materials you need to complete the task?
- Do you have enough time to complete the task?
- Do you know how to use the space, materials and tools to complete the task?
- Have you thought about how you will evaluate the product at the end?

END-ON EVALUATION OF PROCEDURES

Thinking back to how the product was made:

- Did you have enough time?
- Could you have organized your time better?
- Did you have enough space?
- Could you have organized your space in a better way?
- Did you do things in the best order?
- Could you have done things in a better order?
- Did you know enough about the tools and materials you used?
- Would you have benefited by knowing more about these?

Evaluating the products and the procedures made in design and technology is an essential skill for all primary school pupils. It may involve an element of self criticism so it has to be approached sensitively by the teacher. There are many sub-skills to be taught in a progressive manner throughout the primary school. At the same time there are some general principles which can be employed by the teacher at all times. The following is an adaptation of a set of guiding principles for successful encouragement of evaluating devised by a group of teachers.

Figure 2.6   General principles for encouraging primary school pupils to evaluate. Adapted from Johnsey (1995d)

- Value children's responses and opinions.
- Create an atmosphere in the classroom of trust and respect for others' opinions.
- Help children to see that self criticism is a virtue rather than an admission of failure.
- Give children time for reflection before asking for evaluations.
- Ask searching questions about the product and processes involved when appropriate.
- Encourage pupils to ask their own questions by providing examples.
- Promote group work in making evaluations. Sharing ideas leads to greater objectivity and puts less emphasis on personal success or failure.
- Encourage oral responses where children find writing tedious or difficult.
- Provide tape recorders to increase motivation.
- Encourage children to be aware of the purpose for their designed product.
- Set criteria for children which they can use for their own product.
- Encourage children to set out their own criteria against which their products might be judged.

Toolbox skills – Evaluating

Children should develop an ability to:

- relate their evaluations to the specifications and purpose for their product;

- identify the purposes of others' designed products;

- communicate their opinions regarding designed products;

- support their evaluation of products with reasoned argument;

- carry out investigations of products in a scientific way including using skills such as:

  observing;
  measuring;
  identifying and controlling variables;
  gathering evidence;
  recording information systematically;
  analysing data;
  drawing conclusions;

- identify and attempt to eliminate bias in making subjective assessments of products;

- carry out opinion surveys and consumer tests;

- critically consider their own designing and making procedures.

3: Researching the Task and its Possible Solutions

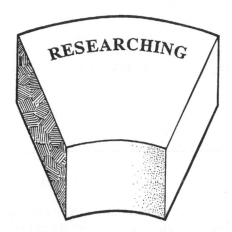

Introduction

Researching is a design process skill which has not been fully recognized or examined in the primary school curriculum. It is a skill particularly suited to the primary school pupil because it can both enhance learning as well as provide the basis for a well designed product. Pupils carrying out design-related research will be gathering information and skills which might support the design task. It can take place at any time after a design task has been defined but will most often be carried out in the early stages. Information found while researching will inform the remainder of the design task. There is evidence to show that pupils will generally not choose to carry out their own research, preferring to base their ideas on what they already know (Johnsey, 1995a). It is by carrying out suitable research activities, however, that the quality of the pupil's learning as well as the design product can be enhanced.

The skill of researching can take many forms, some of which have been discussed already. Examples of researching skills are:

- learning how to use a tool or a construction technique;
- carrying out a science investigation;
- conducting a questionnaire;
- using reference media (books, video, CD ROM etc);
- asking an expert (sometimes the teacher) for advice;
- finding out how problems have been solved by others;
- evaluating designed products;
- making observations.

Considering Research in a Broad Sense

Researching skills have been described in the National Curriculum for England and Wales (DfE, 1995) as *focused practical tasks* or within a part of *investigating, disassembling and evaluating tasks*. However, the important skill of researching should be seen in a broader sense as contributing to the complete process of designing and making.

The Design and Technology Association (DATA) argues in its Guidance Material for Key Stages 1 and 2 (DATA, 1995a) that the three types of activity:

- investigative, disassembly and evaluative activities (IDEAs);
- focused practical tasks (FPTs);
- design and make assignments (DMAs),

should be 'inter-related, with the IDEAs and FPTs supporting and enriching the DMAs'.

They go on to say that 'in a sense the IDEAs and the FPTs involve and ensure focused teaching within a design and make task'.

It is this *supportive* role that pupils carry out when they are researching and it is within the research work that the teacher has a major responsibility to teach. The view that the design and make activity is central to children's development within the subject is a sound one and underpins the arguments for teaching design and technology developed in this book.

Case Study – Umbrellas

A group of children who were studying a topic on The Weather became interested in the idea of protection from the rain. Their teacher asked them to invent something for keeping the rain off her own four year old daughter Zoe as she walked to nursery school each morning.

After discussion with their teacher the children decided to begin their research by investigating umbrellas. They looked at a wide variety of these, noting the mechanisms used to erect the canopy and the materials used in construction. They even investigated cocktail umbrellas as part of their information gathering.

Their teacher realized that the group might want to use wooden dowel rod as part of their solution so she took the opportunity to teach them how to saw this safely using a bench hook and Junior hacksaw.

The children were also interested in looking through the fabrics box in the classroom in search of suitable waterproof materials for their umbrellas. After trying out some of these materials by watching drops of water soak into them they decided to use polythene from bin liners instead.

Some of the children wanted to make folding mechanisms for their umbrella so their teacher showed them how to make simple hinges using pieces of fabric and glue.

The finished products varied in style and quality and were carefully evaluated both by the pupils themselves and Zoe on the next rainy morning.

This case study illustrates a number of ways in which pupils can carry out design-related research. In some instances the research involved evaluating others' design products (umbrellas), while at other times the 'finding out' was more to do with learning something from an expert (being taught how to saw dowel rod safely). It was the children themselves who chose to 'research' the contents of the fabric box and carry out their own science experiment on the waterproofness of various fabrics.

Case Study – Gerbil Cage

Darren and Mark were particularly interested in pets and had been observing the two gerbils which were kept in the year group area between two classrooms. Their teacher, Mrs Bently, suggested that they might like to design and make a model of a new improved gerbil cage using the materials available in the classroom. The boys could make the cage full size as though they were going to show it to a manufacturer who could make it in the correct materials.

The two had already inadvertently carried out some of their research by observing the behaviour and habits of the school gerbils. They noticed how the nest was made at the end of a tunnel through the bedding and they knew how the pets enjoyed exercise.

This research was now extended by a visit to the school library and an afternoon spent reading about gerbils and other similar caged pets. The boys came back armed with some notes and lots of ideas to incorporate into their design for the cage.

This study of the beginning of a design and make task demonstrates two more types of research tasks which might be carried out by primary pupils. The task of observing the gerbils' behaviour might be labelled as a science activity while the use of reference books to gather information clearly employs language skills. Either research activity could have been extended or formalized by the teacher as part of the pupils' study in other areas of the curriculum.

Design-Related Research as an Effective Way of Learning

In the case studies outlined above the examples of research by the pupils have been carried out with a purpose in mind – that is, to complete the design task which had been set. The pupils were learning skills, knowledge and understanding often found in other areas of the primary curriculum and then applying what they had learnt in a meaningful context. Anecdotal evidence and common sense would suggest that pupils' learning would be enhanced when accomplished in this way rather than when it was with a less obvious purpose. Furthermore the application of knowledge and skills in a new situation ie the design task, is often the best test of whether learning has been truly achieved. Design and technology, then, can be seen as a powerful vehicle for effective learning in the primary school. The question of whether this research should be structured and teacher led or if it should be introduced when the needs of the design task dictate this, is discussed later in this section.

Research to Support the Quality of the Designed Product

Design and Technology is very much about children applying their personal skills knowledge and understanding to new situations in which they remix these creatively to achieve a designed product. If their previous experience is limited then we might expect a limited response to the design task. The experience children possess, however, can be enhanced by the teacher by encouraging design related research which directly supports the task in hand. It is quite natural for an inexperienced child who has been presented with a design task to want to get on and produce something as quickly as possible. Many primary aged children would choose naturally to plan as they are making and to base their designs on what they already know. They tend not to choose to carry out their own research. The teacher, therefore, will often be the one who suggests the research to be carried out and will often plan a short programme of activities to promote this. This often gives the teacher control over a part of the design process. It is a time when children can work under close supervision, perhaps using a set of instructions in some form or other. Eventually more experienced children will learn to plan and carry out their own research in which their own preferences and interests are expressed.

Most design tasks could demand a broad range of knowledge and skills from the pupil so the teacher will have to be selective in setting the research tasks. There is a possibility that the research tasks chosen will have a large influence on the designed products the children produce.

Case Study – Chocolate Boxes

A teacher wanted a group of children to design and make a new kind of packaging for chocolates. The children would use simple flat card and glue for the outer box and decide on the inner packaging to protect the delicate chocolates. She considered what kind of research the children might carry out and decided to begin with a survey of chocolate boxes already on the market. The children looked at the box shapes, external graphic designs and the protective packaging inside.

In addition to this survey, the teacher introduced a series of short maths activities in which the children made various three-dimensional boxes from card and glue. They were taught how to cut and score the card and about the importance of flaps for gluing. They made cuboids, triangular prisms and pyramids. Armed with these experiences the children went on to design and make their own 'new' chocolate boxes, using combinations of the ideas they had already tried.

In this example the pupils might be expected to be influenced by the type of three dimensional boxes they produced in their 'maths activities'. It would be up to the teacher to encourage them not to simply reproduce a box they had already made but to try to invent something different. Also there are plenty of other choices the children have to make regarding the graphics on the box and the packaging inside, to make the task sufficiently open-ended.

Perhaps this example illustrates more clearly the difference between a lay or professional designer and the pupil designer. The pupil designer must learn to design and make in an increasingly better way while sometimes sacrificing the ability to be completely creative. It is the lay or professional designer who is relatively unconstrained by the educational process.

Introducing Research as and When it is Required

One way in which the teacher-led research can be made to have less of an influence on the pupil's designed product is to introduce this as and when it is required within the design task. A pupil who sets out to make a chocolate box might request a knowledge of how to make a triangular pyramid from a card net. The teacher then might be able to teach this skill there and then. There are a number of problems with this approach:

- The pupil may not be aware of the possibilities for making unusual three dimensional shapes from card. Triangular prisms may not be part of the pupil's knowledge and therefore no such request will be made.
- The teacher would have to be on hand to discuss this possibility with the pupil and in a busy classroom this opportunity may be missed.
- Teaching one skill to an individual child is a fairly inefficient way to cater for the whole class especially when there may be a larger group who eventually would request the same thing.
- The pupil may prefer to rely on the knowledge already possessed and 'play safe' by making an ordinary cuboid for the box.

There will be times when a teacher has the opportunity to teach a skill as and when required in a design task, perhaps to an individual child, but more can be achieved by building design related research into an overall programme in a structured way.

An important feature of teacher-led design-related research is that the child should have been introduced to the design task before the research is carried out. This will provide a purpose for the learning which will go on. The activities of researching and making the product should be fairly closely linked in time. It would be a mistake for instance to make mathematical card models in isolation in the autumn term and then not make the chocolate boxes until next term. It would be much better to introduce the design task one day and embark upon some related research soon afterwards and then to continue designing and making the next day or perhaps the following week so that the skills and knowledge learnt have not been forgotten or seen as irrelevant.

Evaluating Others' Design Products as Part of Research

If children need to gather information which will enhance their designing and making then one useful source will be in studying the designed products of others. This will be especially helpful if the products being evaluated bear some relevance to the design task the children are about to embark upon. For instance a child who is about to design and make a model table using corrugated card and art straws would learn much useful information by looking closely at a collection of real tables. Their appearance and function could be considered and the way in which the legs are fixed on might be of interest. A group of children about to design and make models of playground apparatus for a local park might spend some time making a survey of apparatus already in existence and evaluating its effectiveness.

Strategies for Encouraging Children to Evaluate the Designed Products of Others

- Encourage children to discuss the purpose for a product. Try to define the set of problems which were being solved.
- Encourage them to put themselves in the place of the designer. Ask 'What were his/her intentions?'.
- Encourage close observation of others' products. Use all the senses.
- Make observational drawings.
- Use aids to observation such as hand lenses.
- Make cartoon strips to show a sequence of actions where this is relevant.
- Help pupils to focus their observations on to relevant parts of the whole.

- Compare items which have a similar function in a collection i.e. a collection of different types of can opener etc.
- Identify mystery objects.
- Compare products from other cultures and times.
- Focus on the materials used for construction and why these, in particular, were used.
- Focus on such features as shape, mechanisms, use of energy and the way the product is controlled.

Many more practical strategies for encouraging an interest in objects made by people can be found in *Learning From Objects* (Durbin *et al.*, 1990).

Toolbox Skills – Researching

Children should develop an ability to:

- learn how to use tools safely and appropriately;
- learn how to employ construction techniques;
- follow written or diagramatic instructions;
- carry out science investigations (e.g. into the properties of appropriate materials for construction);
- conduct opinion surveys (e.g. to assess people's needs);
- draw relevant information from various media e.g.:

  books;
  video;
  CD ROM etc.;

- find out information from other people (e.g. the teacher);
- find out how others have solved problems in the past;
- evaluate designed products.

4:   Generating Ideas and Modelling Outcomes

Generating Ideas for Outcomes

At some point in the design process pupils will need to consider a number of possible products that they might make in order to satisfy the design task. They will be generating ideas for outcomes. A pupil who is generating ideas for the outcome of a design task will be imagining what might be, initially, through mental images. These images will represent possible outcomes for the design activity and may be discussed, sketched or represented in other ways. In the early stages there will often be more than one design outcome envisaged in the mind's eye, though pupils often only reveal a small number of these.

The generation of ideas will naturally occur as soon as the pupil becomes aware of the design task. The list of possibilities will be extended and modified while research is carried out and even while preparations are made for making. Pupils often hold on to one of the first ideas that come into their heads and often need to be persuaded to consider other options.

Strategies for Encouraging Children to Generate Design Ideas:

PEER GROUP DISCUSSION

A lot of useful ideas come to light if the teacher allows some time for a group of children to discuss their ideas among themselves. Some members of the group may be heavily influenced by their friends and accept their suggestions. Careful grouping can be used to avoid this happening too often.

BRAINSTORMING

The whole class or a group can be involved in brainstorming. This is often best conducted by the teacher if the pupils lack experience in this. The idea is that having introduced the problem the children are encouraged to suggest as wide a range of ideas as possible. None of these are accepted or rejected initially. The suggestions can be humorous, impractical, bizarre or made with serious intent. Brainstorming should be fun and can be carried out at a furious pace! The plan is that each suggestion might prompt a new idea so even the impractical ones can give rise to a more practical one later.

As a preliminary to the brainstorming session a teacher might ask all pupils to jot down some ideas first. The teacher needs to engender an atmosphere of trust and acceptance so that all children are encouraged to take part. As chairperson the teacher can include pupils who might be reluctant to take part by asking them for a suggestion directly. Those that tend to dominate discussions can be taught to allow others to participate. The suggestions can be gathered on the blackboard thus allowing some pupils to remember earlier suggestions.

DOODLING

If pupils are asked to make informal sketches or doodles to represent their initial ideas then commitment to each idea will be minimal and yet the pupil will have time to consider more than one idea. The sketches and doodles are not a substitute for a more formal design drawing that might come later.

MAKING A LIST OF POSSIBLE IDEAS

The act of writing ideas down in note form often gives children the chance to consider carefully.

CREATING A 'SPIDER' DIAGRAM LINKING INITIAL IDEAS

This technique is often used by teachers when they plan a cross-curricular topic to show how a variety of ideas link together. Often too many ideas are produced and the final plan has to be edited.

USING TEACHER-PUPIL QUESTIONING TECHNIQUES

Teachers can often tease out design ideas if they ask suitable questions of their pupils.

- Can you think of some more suitable design ideas?
- Would this idea suit the person it is made for?
- Does this idea suit all the purposes that your product is to be made for?
- Can you think of some quite different ideas too?

Toolbox Skills – Generating Ideas

Children should develop an ability to:

- initially maintain an open mind on the possibilities for designing and making;
- think beyond their first ideas;
- brainstorm ideas alone or with others;
- make a series of quick sketches or doodles to express a range of design ideas.

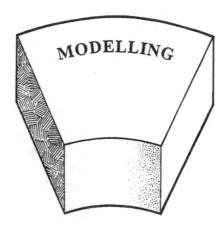

Modelling Ideas

The word model or modelling has a number of meanings and these can lead to some confusion. Some people understand modelling as the *making* of the designed product. 'The children did some modelling with card boxes today'. Others use the word to describe the finished product. 'The finished model was very effective and eye-catching'. Sometimes we talk about *modelling* materials such as clay or papier mâché. Modelling is in fact a much broader activity used in design and technology to describe part of the preparation for making a part or all of a product.

'Modelling is the ability we have to make one thing stand for another.'
(Outterside, 1993)

Children will be modelling if they form some representation of the product they might make and can manipulate this so as to explore and develop it's potential. This 'representation' (which technically is called the 'model') can take many forms such as the following:

- hand gestures to show the form of something;
- a discussion about what something might be like;
- a drawing or painting;
- the forming of the raw materials available into temporary arrangements;
- a paper or card mock-up; etc.

Many of the products of primary design and technology are models themselves – for instance a scale model of a kitchen layout or a full scale card model of a gerbil cage might be the end product of a classroom design task but could be used as a preparation for making the real thing. For the purposes of this book, modelling will refer to the production of preparatory 'models' which can be manipulated before the child's final product is made.

Modelling is to do with firstly seeing things in the 'mind's eye'. It is worth considering the problems that children will encounter when trying to model the products of design and technology. Firstly they need to develop the ability to imagine things that already exist but which are not in front of them. To be able to picture an object which is familiar but which may be stored in a cupboard, out of sight, might present a difficult task for some very young children.

The next stage is to be able to manipulate that image, to turn it around in the mind's eye and perhaps change its form slightly. Finally we will expect children to imagine things which do not yet exist and to manipulate these in the mind. All this must be done before we can expect children to represent these images as drawings or three-dimensional mock-ups. It is not surprising sometimes, that the design drawings children make often bear little resemblance to the products they finally make.

There are many ways in which we might expect children to take images and manipulate them in order to model their ideas. The following are some of the strategies which primary school children can be encouraged to use. At times some of these can replace the conventional design drawing as a way of preparing for making the products of design and technology.

Strategies for Encouraging Children to Take Part in Modelling Ideas:

DISCUSSION

Pupils can work out a lot of their ideas by talking about them to others. In explaining a mental image to others children can explore that image and make modifications to it. Often discussion can be followed by some form of recording of ideas.

MAKING GESTURES

Children naturally describe many of their mental images by using bodily gestures as they talk about them.

Case Study – Jack-in-the-box

Lisa had suddenly thought of the idea of making a toy Jack-in-the-box for her brother. She was explaining her idea to a friend. She had a box in her hand and had decided that the Jack would be fixed on a stick and fit inside the box. She showed her friend how the box would have flaps on top which opened as the Jack shot out. She was able to demonstrate this action by using her hands to represent the flaps on the box. With a great deal of gesturing she was able to demonstrate how the model would work.

Hand gestures can describe the dimensions and shape of a model and how parts of it function and move. The method is a quick and effective way of communicating ideas to others and of manipulating an image held in the mind's eye.

DRAWING

Teachers should be clear in their minds about the different purposes for children's drawings in design and technology. These purposes might include:

(1) a way of recording a detailed observation of products designed by others;
(2) producing a record of what has been made by the child;
(3) a method of planning the sequence of actions needed in making the product;
(4) a way of listing the materials and tools required;
(5) a way of developing graphic symbols which might be used as part of the designed product e.g. the logo for a sports shirt;
(6) a way of communicating the child's ideas about what will be made;
(7) a way of modelling ideas as a preparation for making.

When teachers ask children to make a design drawing, as a preparation for making a product, they often have (6) in mind. This frequently gives rise to a problem which has been identified by many teachers.

'I don't think they need to draw and plan at five. I think they want to make it first and possibly record and draw it afterwards. They don't know what it looks like before they've made it. To see it before you've done it, that's hard.'

Teacher's comment in Anning (1993)

'I encourage them to draw their designs before they make a model, but I have to admit that the designs that they make at the beginning, however fantastic they look, very often the end product isn't like that at all. The original drawing bears no relationship to what the children finally produce. I think that what actually happens is that they are re-designing as they go along all the time, as they are making things . . . I think adults are the same. When they start making things up, often their original ideas are modified drastically, once they get working.'

Teacher's comment in Anning (1993)

This problem is more easily understood if the drawings that children make early on in their design and make task are seen as part of *modelling activities* rather than as final design drawings. If we understand that a model is a temporary representation of the final product then it would be quite natural for that model to be changed as the designing and making proceeds. In reality children will make a drawing of what they imagine they might make and then move on to using the real materials of construction – which in turn become the basis for the new model of what might exist. Children very rarely refer back to their design drawing because they soon become redundant and of no further use – their modelling has moved on.

Teachers might consider the idea of encouraging children to make sketches and drawings *while* they are making rather than merely before making. These intermediate, modelling drawings would be based on the part-finished product and will help the child imagine how to complete the task.

Anning (1993) suggests that teachers often fail to teach the skills of drawing in the primary classroom. 'More usually, drawing is seen as a servicing agent for the "real" work of writing stories – *"When you've finished your writing, draw your picture".'* While skills such as handwriting, the use of a hand lens or bending lengths of wire might be demonstrated by the teacher, those of drawing are most often not. The skills in making a rapid series of sketches – so useful as a modelling skill in design and technology – are often down-graded in favour of 'aiming for a perfect end-product' in a neat drawing or painted picture.

Often teachers will resort to asking children to draw what they have already made. This will certainly help them to develop useful drawing skills and is clearly much easier for the child than drawing something which does not yet exist. Such a drawing, however, is not a design drawing nor a modelling tool. It does highlight the need for children to be able to imagine, in concrete terms, what they are about to draw. It makes a great deal of sense, therefore, to introduce children to the materials they might use in their constructions before they are expected to make drawings or sketches. If this is done, they may find it easier to model their ideas by both using the materials themselves in temporary positions *and* making suitable drawings.

The drawings that children make can take a variety of forms. Teachers will want to ensure that experience is gained in a wide variety of media and techniques so that the most appropriate ones can be chosen to suit a particular task.

Types of 'drawing' which might be suitable for modelling ideas in design and technology:

- sketches
- doodles
- painting
- cartoon strips
- plan drawings
- scale drawings
- exploded drawings
- cross-sectional drawings
- perspective drawings
- isometric projections
- plan, side elevation and end elevations
- computer aided drawing.

MOCK-UPS

A mock-up is a replica of the final product which is made of inexpensive, easily shaped material such as card or paper. For instance the mock-up might represent the mechanism of a simple toy before it is made out of wood. If the mechanism can be made to work partially in card then much time will be saved before it is made in more resistant materials. Sometimes a mock-up of only a part of a model might be made.

Case Study – Electric Motor Powered Vehicle

Lucy and Jane wanted to make a vehicle which was powered by an electric motor. In order that they understood how the belt and pulley mechanism worked their teacher suggested they model the system on a simple upturned cardboard box. The two girls fixed a drinks can on an axle and attached this to the upturned box which acted as a temporary chassis. The motor and elastic band were held in place by hand while the battery was connected. In this way the children could determine where to best place the motor in relation to the drinks can drive wheel. They found that if the elastic band was too tight it slowed the motor and if it was too slack it slipped on the can.

Mock-ups are ideal for deciding on the relative positions of parts of a model such as the moving parts of a pop-up greetings card.

PAPER PATTERNS

A paper pattern is a kind of mock-up. When articles such as clothing are made from fabric it is often necessary to cut the cloth from a paper pattern. The idea of a paper pattern can be used as an excellent modelling strategy when pupils design and make in fabrics or other materials.

Case Study – Finger Puppets

A group of children were making some simple finger puppets so that they could illustrate the story of Little Red Riding Hood. They were able to try out a variety of ideas and shapes for puppets by using coloured tissue paper which they stapled quickly together. A number of these were discarded in favour of a better shape or colour and some of them were altered slightly with a quick snip of the scissors. The children were able to experiment with the puppet forms without spending too much time on it and without wasting valuable fabric.

Paper patterns can be used when children:

- design and make a full scale school bag;
- design and make a new school tie;
- design and make a small scale shopping bag;
- design and make a small purse for a relative;
- design and make a protective apron for a toddler.

The use of a paper pattern for modelling purposes is especially helpful when the product is a three-dimensional shape such as a hat. The paper can act as a flexible fabric and be cut to fit the shape of the head exactly.

ANNOTATING A SCRIPT

In some instances an annotated script or cartoon sequence can act as a model for part of a product.

Case Study – Story Box

Some Year 3 children were asked to make a 'story box' for a popular story which was to be read to a group of Reception class children in the same school. The story box would be full of props which would be drawn out and act as visual stimuli as the story was told. The children were encouraged to model their ideas for the props by taking a photocopy of the story and making short notes in the margin. These annotations indicated which visual model was required and when it should be produced during the story. The children even noted the sound effects they wanted as the props were produced.

This method of modelling ideas could be used when children illustrate a poem with a puppet play or use computer control technology to work bulbs and buzzers in a sequence of actions. For instance a cartoon strip could be used to describe the sequence of actions at a model car park barrier. This could then be translated into a programme of action controlled by a computer.

USING MOULDABLE MATERIALS

Mouldable materials such as Plasticine or modelling clay can be used to produce a model for a product which is to be made later in more durable materials. Children can 'practise' making tile designs using Plasticine or clay before going on to make a fired clay tile. The shape of a skittle for a game could be modelled in Plasticine before it is made more permanently in wood.

Case Study – Inflatable

A class of children had made a visit to the local swimming pool and were involved in designing an improved pool of their own. James and Stewart wanted to design an interesting inflatable for the pool. The class, as a whole, were working on a scale model for the new pool so a model inflatable could be made to scale.

The boys modelled their ideas using Plasticine. They tried a dinosaur, a whale and a dolphin shape before settling on a turtle. They used the Plasticine model turtle as a former upon which to build layers of papier mache. Their final product was a papier mache shell which they could paint in the colours of their choice and which could be placed on show in the model swimming pool.

This case study illustrates how a 'model' for a designed product can sometimes be used in the construction of the product itself. In some instances the 'model' can be turned into the final product as the next example shows.

USING THE MATERIALS OF CONSTRUCTION TO MODEL IDEAS

One of the most natural ways of modelling ideas in design and technology is when children handle the materials they will use in construction and hold these in temporary arrangements in order to develop their ideas. Children will often pick up a sheet of card, for instance, and curve it into various shapes while discussing a possible product with their partner. They might point to parts of the material as they imagine features which might be cut from or marked on it.

Case Study – Carnival Trolley

Karla had already made her trolley using a card box lid with wheels and axles following instructions from the teacher. She was now thinking how to build a decorative carnival float onto the model trolley. She had chosen the theme of Snow White and the Seven Dwarfs and wanted to build a canopy over the trolley. She held a sheet of A4 card over the trailer and curved it so it would fit somewhat like a gypsy caravan. She held it here for a few seconds while she imagined where Snow White would sit and how she would be seen. In her mind's eye the A4 card became two supporting strips, one at each end of the trolley with a viewing space in the middle. She began to cut the strips from the card.

USING A PARTIALLY COMPLETED PRODUCT AS THE MODEL

It is clear that a half finished product acts as a modelling tool for the completion of the product. For instance a child who has partially completed a model table lamp for a doll's house will use the partially finished model to imagine what the final thing will be like. It is quite natural, then, to expect children to change their minds about the final product in the light of this intermediate modelling experience. Modelling, therefore, should not be seen as something which occurs only before making but an activity which continues until making is complete.

USE OF CONSTRUCTION KITS

Construction kits can be assembled and modified relatively quickly and so make useful modelling tools. Often the construction kit is used to make a final product in which case it falls into the category of construction materials and components but when the kit is used as a preparation for making something in a more permanent form then it can be described as a modelling tool. There are some difficulties in asking children to make a final product out of normal classroom materials that is based on a model made with a construction kit. The kit model is likely to be so sophisticated that the permanent product will be a poor reproduction of this. A much more valuable modelling function of a kit is to experiment with various mechanisms so that these can be transferred to the designed product.

Case Study – Toy Crane

As part of a topic on the building site a group of children were interested in making toys that represented some of the machinery they had seen. Martin and Julie wanted to make a simple crane out of wood strips with a winding mechanism. They found that every time the load was wound up on its hook it would quickly fall to the ground when the handle was released. With their teacher's help they realized they could use something called a ratchet to prevent this happening. In order to understand the way the ratchet worked they used a construction kit to reproduce the mechanism. This enabled them to model the best arrangement for their own partly completed toy. They eventually made their own ratchet mechanism using a wooden wheel on to which they glued lolly sticks.

In some instances the components of a kit can be used to support a mechanism which is being developed for the final product. For instance a kit can be set up to hold a propeller and elastic band mechanism while it is tested for smooth running and the arrangement of elastic bands and drive shafts is worked out.

Use of Information Technology as a Modelling Tool

Spreadsheets, simulations and graphics packages are all modelling tools associated with information technology. It is the drawing and painting packages, however, which present the greatest potential for assisting in modelling in design and technology in the primary school. When appropriate, pupils might choose to use the draw facility on a graphic package to experiment with the design of a product. Lines and colours can often be changed quickly using such a package and there is potential for unprecedented geometrical accuracy in using some of the basic facilities. Pupils should be encouraged to ask themselves if using IT will help or hinder them. There are many types of drawing that would be much easier to execute using a simple pencil and paper. The constraints of using a basic graphics package will almost certainly restrict the kind of model which is being planned.

Modelling for Food Products

Modelling ideas for designing and making food products throws up a set of intriguing questions. How can the taste and texture of a food product be modelled? Is it possible to use anything but the food ingredients themselves in the modelling process? There are aspects of food technology which can be modelled such as the appearance and presentation of the food but finding a 'representation' for taste and texture becomes more problematic. Raw food can be tasted in advance and a cooked dish can be sampled while it is cooking. Children can effectively model their ideas for food products by remembering the effect and taste of recipes and ingredients they have experienced in the past and imagining how these might be combined in the future.

Summary

It should not be assumed that a design drawing is the only way in which to prepare to make a product in design and technology. Clearly the concept of modelling needs to be considered in a broader sense and a variety of modelling strategies developed for use by primary aged pupils. The important thing is that images can be manipulated and subsequently communicated prior to and during the making process.

Toolbox Skills – Modelling

Children should develop an ability to:

- imagine in the mind's eye;
- describe what is in the mind's eye;
- use hand gestures to represent aspects of a product;
- sketch, draw or represent an imagined product through other graphic methods;
- make representations of a product using mouldable materials such as Plasticine, clay, Plaster of Paris;
- use construction kits to represent the appearance or function of a product or parts of a product they might make.

5:   Making the Product

Planning and Organizing in Preparation for Making

Children who are *planning* to make will be looking ahead and deciding how to proceed during the making/evaluating stages. Planning may involve deciding how to proceed for varying lengths of time such as the next minute or so or to the end of the whole task. Planning, in this instance, does not refer to the generating and modelling of ideas (sometimes referred to as 'designing something').

Pupils will be *organizing* their resources when they arrange their workspace to suit the task (tidy up etc), collect appropriate materials and tools and allocate jobs to different group members.

The idea of planning and organizing the making stage presupposes a neat break between designing activities and making activities. It has been argued that this often does not occur, the designing skills mixing in extricably with the making skills. Once this has been recognized, however, there will be an optimum time when the teacher can encourage pupils to make some plans as to how making might proceed. Often a lesson will begin in which the major task is making and it is this that can be planned carefully by primary aged pupils. Pupils will need to consider:

- the materials they will use in construction;
- the tools required to cut, shape and join the materials;
- the skills they will require to complete the task;
- the time they have available;
- the space they have available;
- the sharing of responsibilities with a partner;
- the sequence in which the making will proceed.

Strategies for Encouraging Children to Plan and Organize

Less experienced children will find it easier to plan over shorter periods, while as children reach the top of the primary school they can be expected to plan well ahead. A brief discussion about what might be done in a single lesson would be appropriate for a group of 6 year-olds, while a year 6 child might be encouraged to plan ahead for 4 or 5 sessions over a period of weeks.

MAKING LISTS OF MATERIALS AND TOOLS THAT WILL BE REQUIRED

Children can be encouraged to plan ahead by considering the materials which might need to be collected from home for instance. Children can make their own lists or a class list can be made on the blackboard. Many young children will find it difficult to imagine all the materials which are available. They will benefit a great deal from being able to see and possibly handle the materials they might use. Perhaps these can be stored in a box or cupboard into which the children might look before deciding what to use. The teacher might consider developing a catalogue of construction resources in picture form which can be browsed by children before and during the designing of their products. The children themselves might be involved in cutting pictures from magazines to make this resource.

CARRYING OUT GROUP DISCUSSIONS

Much planning will happen naturally as children discuss with their partners how to proceed. Teachers can provide a formal occasion when this happens thus enabling children to consider their procedures more carefully. It would be a good idea to begin each teaching session in this way when it is appropriate.

MAKING CARTOON SEQUENCES OF ACTION

Children will benefit from thinking carefully about the order in which they might do things. The natural tendency will be for children to decide these kinds of things as making proceeds but as they become more experienced they will be able to plan further ahead. Producing a cartoon sequence with about four or five frames is a simple and interesting way for children to plan ahead. If the cartoon frames are made on pre-cut rectangles of paper these can later be glued on to a larger sheet in the correct sequence. Children will have the chance, before gluing, to insert extra frames or to rearrange the sequence in the light of their increasing knowledge of the task.

MAKING SEQUENTIAL LISTS WITH TIMES

Producing a written sequence of actions together with estimated times taken is a further skill that children can learn. These kinds of plans can be reviewed on a regular basis as making proceeds. A diary system might be adopted if children know they have so many lessons in which to complete their task.

USING A PLANNING SHEET

The teacher can often design a planning sheet which suits the particular design and make assignment in hand.

Figure 2.7 Example of a planning sheet for making in design and technology

PLANNING TO MAKE			
My design task is			
The materials I will need			
The tools I will need			
A cartoon to show the order I will work in			
I will need special help with			

Inevitably with children of primary school age, much of the planning will occur as the project proceeds. There is a limit to how far anyone can plan ahead in a task which is open-ended. As children progress through the primary school, however, they can be encouraged to plan and organize to a greater degree.

Toolbox Skills – Planning and Organizing to Make

Children should develop an ability to:

- think ahead when considering resources such as materials, space and time;
- think ahead when considering the sequence of their actions;
- record their plans by discussion, drawing or writing;
- review their plans as the design and make assignment proceeds

---

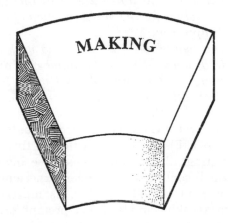

Making

Pupils will be making when they are involved in using tools, materials and components to produce an outcome. Skills such as drawing or marking, cutting, and joining will be used in making. The act of making might include the modification and improvement of a product through construction or otherwise.

The process skill of making has been shown to be a dominant one especially at primary school level. The process models Figure 1.5 and Figure 1.7 show how making and evaluating go hand in hand and there is evidence to show that *making* promotes and enables many of the other process skills discussed so far (Johnsey 1995b). While children are apparently making, much thinking and decision making will be going on.

Children will be specifying requirements for their projected outcomes, generating ideas, modelling, planning further making and evaluating what they have done.

Case Study – Mobile

Sumina had decided to make a simple mobile with a single balanced rod supporting a cardboard cut-out car hanging at each end. She had drawn and cut out one car for one end of the mobile and had begun the second. While engaged in this task she decided she needed some more ideas about how this car should look. She carried out some simple research by finding an appropriate book from the library and finding a picture of a car she wanted to draw.

Once she had completed the second car and fixed it on the mobile she decided that it would look better if there was another card cut-out hanging in the middle of the mobile. She also decided the mobile would be a present for her brother's birthday in a few weeks time. In doing this she had added to her list of specifications for the product. Her teacher encouraged her to record these new specifications for later use. With these ideas in mind she drew and cut out an aeroplane for the middle section of the mobile and then hung it up to check its appearance.

Part of her on-going evaluation was concerned with checking how well the mobile would spin around. She tested a number of different supporting 'threads' including string, cotton and coloured wool. She found that the sewing thread gave a much better movement than any of the others.

This case study illustrates the close connection between making and a number of other process skills already identified in this Part. Researching, specifying and evaluating all depended on a close involvement with the emerging product which could not have been experienced before making had commenced. The skill of making, then, is inextricably linked with many of the other process skills and is often a prompt for such thinking and reasoning skills. A teacher who recognizes this will be ready to intervene to promote successful strategies for carrying out such skills once making has begun as well as prior to this.

Making Skills

Making involves many sub-skills such as:

- measuring
- marking out
- cutting and shaping
- fitting and assembling
- joining and combining
- finishing.

Add to this list the range of materials from which children will make their products in the primary school and a check list emerges which can be used to check that a scheme of work has achieved a balance in these areas.

Figure 2.8 Table to show examples of how the various making sub-skills relate to the materials used in construction.

MATERIAL	MAKING SKILLS					
	Measuring	Marking out	Cutting & shaping	Fitting & assembling	Joining & combining	Finishing
Paper and card	measuring length of an art straw	drawing a star shape to be cut out	using sissors to cut paper to size curling paper strips with the edge of a pair of sissors	fitting one card tube inside another	gluing a paper hat together/ using sticky tape to join card	painting, crayoning, using a felt pen on paper
Wood	measuring width of strip of wood	marking wood strip to length	sawing wood strips/drilling holes in wood	fitting a dowel into a pre-cut hole	using a hot glue gun to join a wooden wheel on an axle	painting, sanding, coating in polyurethane
Textiles	comparing the area of a sheet of fabric with the hand it has to fit over	using chalk to mark out some felt	using fabric cutting scissors	stuffing a fabric teddy bear	sewing the parts of a simple purse using yarn to create an appliqué pattern on a bag	dying a fabric scarf
Plastics		marking a circle of plastic to make a lid	using a sharp knife to cut thin sheet plastic bending plastic pieces to shape	fitting plastic Lego pieces together	stapling thin pieces of plastic	covering a plastic model with coloured paper
Metals	measuring the length of a piece of wire for an axle		cutting wire with a pair of pliers bending wire into a handle shape	fitting paper fasteners to a model assembling wire axles on to wheels for a vehicle	twisting wire components together	
Food	measuring out volumes of water/weight of butter		slicing cucumber/fruit making bread rolls into suitable shapes	assembling a sandwich	making a pastry mix/ creating a new sandwich filling	arranging food for presentation
Mouldable materials			using a knife to cut clay placing papier mâché on a moulded former	assembling the parts of a clay pot	joining clay slabs with slip	glazing fired clay pot, painting a dried papier mâché product

Teachers can complete the blank table below by entering the year groups and term in which each is represented. An over emphasis on one area or gaps in the children's experiences can thus be identified.

Figure 2.9   Grid to assist in planning a balance in the use of materials and making skills in design and technology

MATERIAL	MAKING SKILLS					
	Measuring	Marking out	Cutting & shaping	Fitting & assembling	Joining & combining	Finishing
Paper and card						
Wood						
Textiles						
Plastics						
Metals						
Food						
Mouldable materials						

MEASURING

Children will be taught to measure quantities in science, maths, geography and other curriculum subjects. The purposes for measuring in design and technology are:

- to avoid wasting materials, e.g. cutting four equal lengths of wood strip from a single piece;
- to obtain a match in size between parts of a model, e.g. to make sure a hat fits on a head;

- to conform to a particular design brief i.e. arrange a flower bed to occupy four square metres;
- to achieve a particular culinary effect, e.g. measuring out the correct quantities for a biscuit mix;
- to use a scale representation in modelling ideas for a product, e.g. drawing a plan of a bedroom which is to be redesigned;
- to test a physical property of a product, e.g. test the strength of a carrier bag by pulling with a Newton meter or measuring how far a paper bridge has deformed.

MARKING OUT

Marking out may be linked to measuring as when a strip of paper is marked to length before being cut. It may also involve the drawing of a shape such as a star which is to be cut out for decoration. The marks might be made with a pencil on card, chalk or dress making pins on fabric or knife marks on a block of butter.

Marking-out skills will include:

- folding paper to divide it into equal parts;
- making small pencil marks to show where a cut should be made;
- drawing straight lines with a pencil and ruler;
- drawing irregular shapes freehand;
- using a sharp instrument to mark plastic (e.g. a compass point);
- marking out fabrics.

CUTTING AND SHAPING

There is a wide range of cutting and shaping tools available in the primary classroom from fingers which can tear pieces of paper to a junior hacksaw for cutting sections of wood. A hole punch can be used for making clean holes in paper or card or a pastry cutter can produce identical circles of pastry for mince pies.

Cutting skills will include:

- tearing irregular shapes;
- using scissors on paper or card;
- using a hole punch;
- using scissors on thin plastics;
- using scissors on fabric;
- tearing along a folded line;
- using a junior hacksaw to cut wood;
- using a pair of pliers to cut wire;
- using a hand drill for making holes in wood or plastic;
- cutting clay;
- cutting food items.

Shaping skills will include:

- folding or bending paper and card in a variety of ways (straight line, scrunching tissue etc);
- scoring card for folding;
- using sandpaper on wood or plastic;
- curling paper strips;
- bending wire with hands or pliers;
- moulding clay or Plasticine;
- shaping items of food such as cutting decorative cucumber slices or using cake moulds.

FITTING AND ASSEMBLING

Fitting involves a process of matching parts of a product for size so that they can be joined or assembled. Assembling involves joining parts of a product without using adhesives or other permanent methods of fixture.

JOINING AND COMBINING

Parts of a product can be joined in permanent or semi-permanent ways. There are a wide variety of ways of joining, some of which are specific to the materials being joined but many others which might be used on any material. Primary children should be allowed to explore different ways of joining and combining rather than being taught hard and fast rules about how this should be done.

Different ways of joining and combining include using:

- adhesives (PVA, hot glue, water based pastes etc);
- sticky tapes (Sellotape, masking tape, double sided sticky tape etc);
- gummed paper, sticky labels;
- paper clips, paper fasteners, drawing pins, small nails
- dress making pins;
- staples (including gun staples);
- string, thread, rope, yarn, flexible wire for tying;
- stitching;
- plaiting and weaving;
- slotting components together e.g. construction kit parts;
- clay slip (for joining clay pieces);
- milk, water, cream, jam etc for joining food products.

Each of these joining media will have a set of skills associated with it. For instance there are certain strategies that children should learn concerning the use of a hot glue gun. Combining food products will involve a knowledge of mixing in different ways. Stitching will require manual skills as well as a knowledge of basic stitch patterns.

FINISHING

Products can be finished in a variety of ways. These will include decorative as well as functional finishes. A brick pattern painted on the wall of a model dolls' house will be decorative while a coat of polyurethane varnish on a balsa wood boat will prevent it becoming waterlogged.

Methods for finishing a product include:

- making marks as decoration or simulation using pencil, pencil crayon, wax crayon, felt pen etc;
- painting using water based paints or appropriate spirit based paints;
- pasting coloured paper etc to cover a surface or filling a gap (cladding);
- printing;
- use of stencils;
- spatter painting or spray painting;
- treating wood products with dilute PVA medium, linseed oil, polyurethane varnish, wood stain etc;
- adding body work to a functioning model e.g. an electric powered vehicle;
- dyeing fabric or yarn as a finishing procedure e.g. tie dyeing, batik etc;
- adding decoration in the form of simple stitching appliqué to fabrics;
- dusting a fairy cake with castor sugar, hundreds and thousands etc;
- providing a textured design to clay, Plasticine or a food product such as pastry;
- reducing texture by smoothing e.g. with sandpaper, a wet sponge on clay or glazing food products.

There is a danger that finishing a designed product might become the most important feature of the design and make process because it will provide a satisfying end-product. In some instances children may be encouraged to spend a disproportionate amount of time 'decorating' their product. There are, however, many other features of a product by which it should be judged such as its function, its fitness for purpose, its environmental impact and, most important of all, its contribution to the child's education.

Making Techniques

There are many interlinked facets to the process skill of making such as a knowledge of materials, the acquisition of tool skills as well as the basic making skills outlined above. In addition to these facets there is a wide range of techniques which children can employ during their making which will be defined later in this book as *Practical Capability*. This includes such knowledge and skills as an understanding of stability, structures and the control of products. These aspects will be discussed more fully in Parts 3 and 4.

Toolbox skills – Making

Children should develop an ability to:

- work with a wide variety of materials and components including construction kits;
- measure length, area, volume, capacity, mass, force (including weight), time, temperature etc. using the appropriate instruments;
- mark out a wide variety of materials with the appropriate tools;
- cut a wide variety of materials with the appropriate tools;
- shape a wide variety of materials with the appropriate tools;
- fit and assemble parts of a product;
- join and combine a wide variety of materials and components using appropriate materials;
- finish products appropriately using appropriate materials and techniques.

Part Three

Knowledge and Understanding in Primary Design and Technology

Introduction

In this Part knowledge and understanding in design and technology will be taken to mean the understanding of a body of facts together with a greater appreciation of certain concepts or 'big ideas' associated with the subject. There are many text books on the market now, and which will exist in the future, which deal in depth with the knowledge and understanding required in primary design and technology. This Part aims to outline that essential knowledge and understanding so that an overview is obtained. Teachers will then have a clearer idea of which areas of knowledge and understanding they need to master at their own level through further reading and by attending in-service courses.

The appreciation and acquisition of practical skills will be dealt with in Part 4 – Practical Capability. That is not to suggest that the two areas are exclusive. Much knowledge and understanding can be gained through carrying out practical activities and many practical skills will be enhanced by a greater understanding of key facts and concepts.

Teaching Knowledge and Understanding

Children's knowledge and understanding in design and technology can be taught through a number of avenues:

- as part of the pupil's design-related research
- through other subject areas

pupils may learn about how a belt and pulley system works in preparation for designing and making their own toy windmill

pupils may learn about electrical circuits in a science lesson

- by completing a
  design and
  make task

  a short bridge-building, problem-solving exercise may lead to a better understanding of structures

- as a one-off,
  isolated lesson

  pupils learn to bake flapjacks from a recipe for the school fair

In Part 2 it was argued that children learn more effectively if they perceive a reason for doing so and that 'reason' could be the completion of a design and make task. The power of design and technology to act as a vehicle for children's learning lies in the use of design-related research for teaching knowledge and understanding. Teachers might like to think how they can weave the teaching of important areas of knowledge and understanding into meaningful design and make tasks rather than teach these in isolation.

Pupils will require a wide range of knowledge and understanding from all areas of the curriculum as well as from outside the formal school curriculum in order to support and enhance their work in design and technology. Some areas of knowledge and understanding, however, form a central feature of the primary design and technology curriculum. These are:

- materials and components;
- control using mechanisms;
- control using electricity;
- structures and forces;
- the use of information technology;
- a study of products and applications;
- quality of designed products;
- health and safety;
- the use of appropriate vocabulary.

1:   Materials and Components

Introduction

The word materials refers to the basic building and construction substances used to make products. Paper, clay and flour are all materials used in design and technology and these are generally treated as consumables. Components are ready-made 'building blocks' with which to make products and these are often reclaimed and reused in the primary classroom. Batteries, bulbs, wheels and construction kit pieces are often thought of as components.

An understanding of the raw materials and components of construction in making designed products is fundamental to the subject. Much of this knowledge is gained intuitively as children design and make with materials. A study of materials and components alone, without a context in which these might be used, is to be avoided.

The basic materials used for design and technology in the primary school are

- paper and card;
- wood;
- plastics;
- metals;
- textiles;
- food;
- adhesives and adhesive tapes.

A few minor materials can be included such as rubber (balloons, elastic bands), glass (marbles), lubricants (soap or oil), mouldable material (clay, plasticine, plaster of paris, papier mâché) etc.

The Form of Materials

Materials can be obtained in various forms. Paper can be bought in tissue, crepe or other forms. Wood can be obtained as sheet material (plywood) or in strip form (1 cm section lengths). Metal is most often used in wire or component form while plastics can be supplied in sheet or solid forms. Many materials can be obtained inexpensively by using recycled containers etc. Thus strips of flexible plastic can be cut from a lemonade bottle and corrugated card can be cut from packing boxes. Textiles can be bought as yarn or sheet fabric and can be formed from a wide variety of materials or substances such as nylon, cotton or wool. Food can be used as basic ingredients (flour) or as already combined substances such as chocolate.

Each form of material can be obtained in further more complex forms such as art straws, card tubes, corrugated plastic sheet or an insulated length of electrical wire. It is at this point that basic materials begin to become components and the boundary between them becomes blurred. Is a length of plastic coated gardener's wire a component or a material and how do we classify a piece of Velcro used to fasten the flap on a small purse?

Components

Components might consist of commercially bought, complete items such as wooden wheels, paper clips or construction kits. They might also be prepared by the teacher especially for a particular activity. Items such as pre-cut dowel rods, crocodile connecting leads and sliced bread might fall into this category. Many of the key features of materials will be studied through children using components. The springiness of metals might be studied through the use of springs, while the flexibility and waterproof qualities of plastics might be understood by the use of plastic tubing in a study of hydraulics. The use of many construction kits will increase children's understanding of the properties and qualities of plastics.

The Properties of Materials

The basic materials such as types of wood or plastic have characteristics which are true for all pieces of that material. All pieces of polythene are waterproof, all pieces of softwood float and all pieces of an apple taste practically the same. However, it would be a mistake to claim that all pieces of wood were strong because strength depends on how much of the material is used. You can walk across a stream on a large felled tree trunk but not necessarily on a thin plank made from the same wood.

This distinction is sometimes a hard one for children to appreciate. Younger, less experienced children will often describe the properties of an *object* rather than the properties of the *material* from which it is made. This appreciation that similar objects have similar properties, however, is a good beginning and should be encouraged.

An understanding of the properties of individual objects requires an appreciation that generalized statements can be made about a wide number of similar things. All hole punches are strong enough to punch through five or six layers of paper. All elastic bands will stretch and return to their original shape exerting a force as they do so.

A step further on from an appreciation that objects have similarities and differences, is an understanding that this is true of the material from which the object is made. Even the smallest piece of kitchen roll paper will soak up water but it might require four or five sheets of the paper to soak up the spilt coffee from a half-full cup. All pieces of rubber can exert a force when stretched but only certain thicknesses of elastic (rubber) bands will exert enough force to drive a model vehicle along a table top.

The strength of a piece of material can be changed, either by adding more of the same material to it, by adding different materials to it or by making it into a stronger shape which is more able to withstand the forces on it. More is said about the strength of materials in the section in this Part on Structures and Forces.

The properties of materials which can be explored by primary school children in design and technology include the following:

- ability to float or sink
- absorbency
- colour
- density or weight for size
- ease with which it can be folded
- ease with which it is cut or shaped
- ease with which the material can be joined by adhesives
- flavour or taste
- flexibility/rigidity
- graininess (of wood or fabrics for instance)
- malleability
- reflective qualities
- springiness (ability to return to original shape)
- strength when being bent
- strength when being squashed
- strength when being stretched
- strength when being twisted
- texture (appearance or feel)
- transparency/opacity
- waterproof properties.

Each property can be explored at different levels of sophistication. A Year 1 child might look at how easily a material can soak up water from a table top and be able to compare two different materials. She might tell her teacher which she would use to mop up spilt milk on a surface. A Year 6 child might test a range of potential materials for absorbency in a more sophisticated way, taking measurements of the volume of water absorbed in millilitres each time. The child might then go on to carry out further tests for other properties before deciding which material to use for an interior car windscreen wiper.

Strategies to Encourage Children to Learn About Materials and Components

The teacher can employ a number of strategies to encourage a greater knowledge of materials and components.

OBSERVATION

Children can be encouraged to observe the properties of materials by having their attention drawn to the way they behave in various circumstances. They might make a study of the flexibility of different plastics in the classroom by completing an observation worksheet:

Figure 3.1   Worksheet on the flexibility of materials

LOOKING AT MATERIALS IN THE CLASSROOM – FLEXIBILITY
- Find out which materials and objects are flexible in the classroom.
- Make a small collection of objects shown in this table.
- Add three objects of your own. (Each object should only be made of one material.)
- Complete the table of results

Object	Material	Is it bendy? not at all a bit a lot	Hold one end of the object still. Measure how far you can move the other end
Plastic ruler			
Wooden ruler			
Rubber			
Plastic tubing			
Pencil			
Metal chair leg			
Blackboard chalk			
Card tube			
Lemonade bottle			

Which is the most flexible object? _____
Which is more flexible wood or the same size plastic? _____

If you had two equal length strips of wood how could you make one more flexible than the other? _____

SCIENTIFIC TESTING

Children might carry out more formal tests on scraps of fabric to discover how waterproof they are. In doing so they will be involved in carrying out a scientific investigation by controlling variables and taking measurements. This knowledge of the materials may then be used to design and make a waterproof hat.

MAKING TO A RECIPE

Children may be asked to make something by following instructions such as a recipe for making shortbread or a workcard which shows how to make a Christmas tree decoration. Armed with this knowledge they may go on to design and make something of their own.

AS PART OF DESIGN-RELATED RESEARCH

Children may prepare themselves for designing and making their own 'glove' puppet by exploring different ways of fixing felt shapes to the fabric of an old sock. They might try PVA adhesive, staples or double sided sticky tape in a simple task directed by the teacher. They then decide which to use on their own model.

EVALUATING THE USE OF DIFFERENT MATERIALS IN PRODUCTS DESIGNED BY OTHERS

Children might list all the different materials used in making a school bag. They can be encouraged to talk about why the materials were chosen, what was special about their properties and what alternatives there might have been. In considering a table lamp, for instance, children might speculate on the effect of using alternative materials such as cardboard, solid iron or Plasticine. Some construction kits are made from a variety of materials. Children might discuss why some parts are made from rigid plastic while others are more flexible.

Figure 3.2 overleaf shows how a designed product can be examined for the different materials used in its construction.

COMBINING AND MIXING MATERIALS TO PRODUCE NEW COMPONENTS OR EFFECTS

Children might be asked to experiment freely with folding tissue paper to find new decorative techniques. They might be asked to combine materials to produce a set of flexible joints for a puppet's limbs. They might investigate adding different ingredients to a basic bread mix in order to decide on the best combination. They might try a number of different finishes on scraps of wood to decide on the best finish for a child's wooden toy.

Figure 3.2   The use of materials in designing and making

MATERIALS FOR DESIGNING AND MAKING

- Look at this picture of a torch;
- Try to find one like it;
- Label each part to show which material you think it is made from.

Complete the following table:

Part of torch	Material it is made from	Why is this material used?
wiring inside	metal	conducts electricity
'lens'		
reflector		
body of torch		
switch slider		
strap		

Describe what would happen if the body of the torch was made from cloth.

Why isn't the 'lens' made from thin wood?

What else could the reflector be made from?

2:   Control in Design and Technology

Introduction

The concept of controlling things is fundamental to designing and making. Many products of design and technology need to be controlled in various ways so that a particular job is done. For instance a puppet is controlled by its strings, a bicycle is controlled by its gears, pedals and handlebars and a robot can be controlled by a computer. The control can be through mechanical means as in a simple can opener or pop-up card or by electrical means as in a torch or a pocket calculator. Many devices are controlled by a combination of mechanisms and electrical circuits.

Children can explore the idea of control by discussing a wide range of everyday devices which make use of it. There are many examples of products in and around the home which are controlled in simple ways. Sometimes a set of movements are controlled, often by employing simple mechanisms. At other times features, such as sound, light and movement can be controlled through the use of electrical switches.

Devices such as corkscrews, scissors, door catches and toilet flushes can all be controlled by various types of lever and pivots. Springs, the force of gravity or human muscles can be used to return any movements which have been made. A pedal cycle brake lever is returned by a strong spring action while a pedal bin lid falls back into place under gravity. A roller blind is a good example of the use of strings to control movement while the handle on a toaster shows how a connecting rod can move something (the slice of bread) at the same time as turning on an electric current. Kitchen scales demonstrate how a linear downward movement of the pan can be translated into a turning movement of a pointer on a scale. Alternatively, the turn of a key in a lock shows how a circular motion can change to the linear one of the bolt.

Simple electrical switches are often all that are needed to control other household devices. A table lamp has a simple switch to control it while a food mixer has a variable speed control. The volume of sound on a radio is controlled by a variable resistor and the central heating system is controlled by a thermostat which senses room temperature before switching the system on or off. More sophisticated electronics are employed when a device is programmable such as a video recorder which can be made to switch on and off at predetermined times.

Control with Mechanisms

Mechanisms are used to control movement in models by mechanical means. There are different kinds of movement which can be controlled and ways of changing one type into another. Some model parts rotate such as wheels and axles or a winding mechanism. Other movements include moving in an arc such as on a model playground swing or linear movements such as a push rod or a string on a puppet. If a cam is used on a model toy then its rotation will make something bob up and down while the linear pull of an elastic band wrapped around an axle will produce a rotation of the wheels.

The main types of mechanism used in primary design and technology include:

- strings and rods;
- wheels and axles;
- levers, linkages and pivots;
- winches/handles;
- pneumatics and hydraulics;
- belts and pulleys;
- cams;
- gears.

STRINGS AND RODS

Strings and rods produce a movement in a line and may be used to control a wide range of movements on a model.

Case Study

Stacey and Jake were exploring the need to reach objects which were at a distance and out of reach. As part of their design-related research they were investigating a mechanical grabber that their teacher had asked them to make. They had made the grabber following a worksheet and were now considering how to control the 'fingers'.

Figure 3.3   The mechanical grabber

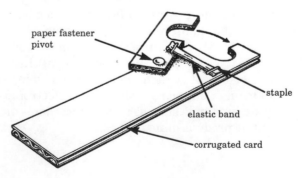

90

Their solution was to use a rod of stiff wire which would push or pull the moving finger. This required another pivot where the rod fixed to the finger and a guide sleeve to keep the rod in place.

Figure 3.4   Controlling the grabber

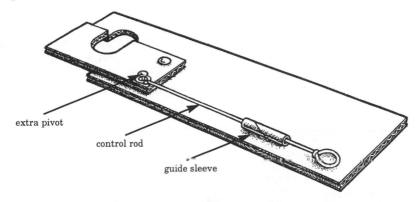

extra pivot

control rod

guide sleeve

A solution involving a string might look like this

Figure 3.5   Controlling the 'hand' with strings

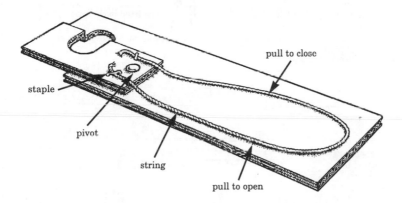

pull to close

staple

pivot

string

pull to open

WHEELS AND AXLES

Wheels and axles constitute a fundamental mechanism in primary design and technology. Rotating parts can be found on pop-up cards, a wide range of vehicles and models such as model fairground rides, windmills and helicopters. The axle can be anything from a paper fastener to a metal spindle cut from a length of straight welding wire. The wheels can be anything from card discs to commercially available plastic moulded wheels with realistic 'tyres'.

The three basic ways of fixing wheels to axles are illustrated overleaf:

The simple idea of fixing a card disc with a paper fastener is suitable for two dimensional work where a disc has to turn for effect on a greetings card for instance. It can be used on three dimensional models of vehicles but would not run very efficiently. A simple alternative might be to use drawing pins fixed through the wheel into a softwood block.

When it comes to making more sophisticated vehicles, an axle passing all the way through the chassis is essential. If the wheel is loose on the axle then it may wobble somewhat and will therefore need a spacer between the wheel and chassis to prevent rubbing. This could be a bead or a short length of tubing which is threaded on to the axle before the wheel. This arrangement will also need a 'stop' to prevent the wheel falling off the end of the axle.

Figure 3.6 Three ways of fixing a wheel to an axle

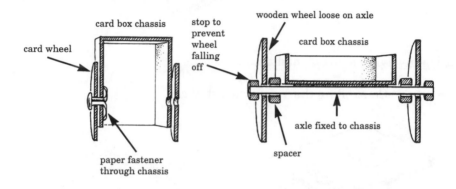

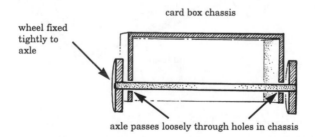

A much more successful arrangement is when the wheel fits snugly on to the axle. This requires no spacer or stops on the end of the axle but does require the hole in the wheel to be about the right size for the axle. Axles which are too small for the hole can have a short length of sticky tape wrapped around them to increase the diameter before fitting tightly on to the axle. Avoid gluing the wheel on since it might need to come off at a later date. This arrangement is essential if the vehicle is to be driven by an electric motor, say, or an elastic band. In these instances the axle will be turned by the source of power, which in turn will rotate the wheels *only* if they are attached.

The following are the basic principles that primary school children might learn about wheels and axles:

Wheels and axles

- Wheels and axles are used in a wide variety of everyday devices;
- A wheel must be as round as possible to run smoothly;
- An axle or spindle must be as straight as possible to run smoothly;
- Wheels should fit at right angles to the axle;
- A thin (card) wheel will not fit so firmly at right angles as a thicker wheel;
- Thin card wheels can be made 'thicker' in a variety of ways.

Figure 3.7   Making wheels thicker

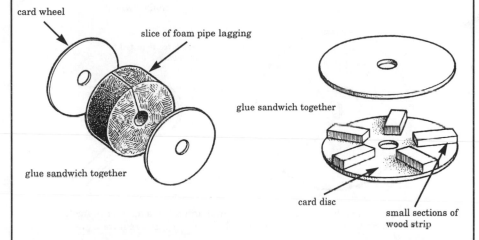

card wheel

slice of foam pipe lagging

glue sandwich together

glue sandwich together

card disc

small sections of wood strip

- The weight of a set of wheels can add considerably to the overall weight of the vehicle;
- On a typical four wheel vehicle, axles should be parallel to each other and opposite wheels should be parallel to each other and the same size as each other for that vehicle to travel in a straight line;
- All rotating parts of a wheel and axle system should be made to run as smoothly as possible. Reducing friction might involve:
    keeping wheels away from the chassis with spacers;
    cutting clean holes for the axles to run in or the wheels to turn on;
    using axles made of smooth material such as polished metal rods;
    using lubricants;
- Friction may need to be increased:
    where the driving force is relatively strong thus making the wheels skid on the 'road' surface
    where the 'road' or wheel surface is particularly smooth
- Larger diameter wheels will move more effectively over a rough surface than smaller ones.

Figures 3.8–3.10 show (a) different diameter wheels, (b) the acceleration in wheels of different diamenter, (c) the effect of different diameter axles

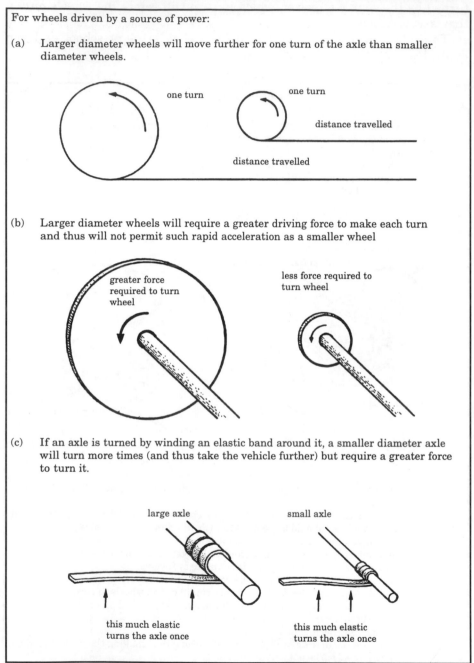

For wheels driven by a source of power:

(a)   Larger diameter wheels will move further for one turn of the axle than smaller diameter wheels.

one turn

one turn

distance travelled

distance travelled

(b)   Larger diameter wheels will require a greater driving force to make each turn and thus will not permit such rapid acceleration as a smaller wheel

greater force required to turn wheel

less force required to turn wheel

(c)   If an axle is turned by winding an elastic band around it, a smaller diameter axle will turn more times (and thus take the vehicle further) but require a greater force to turn it.

large axle

small axle

this much elastic turns the axle once

this much elastic turns the axle once

The effect of drive belts and gearing as well as off-centre and eccentric wheels (cams) are discussed later in this section.

WINCHES AND HANDLES

Winches are simple devices which consist of an axle or drum fitted with a handle and are often used to wind a length of cord or thread on to. A toy crane would use a winch and the handle and drum at the top of a well can be used to wind the bucket up or down. The winch can also drive a belt or gearing system as found on the old wind-up gramophones. A simple winch, with or without a drive belt can be used on a model to produce a rotating movement before the complications of harnessing an electric motor are met. More is said about drive belts and gearing later in this section.

Figure 3.11   Examples of simple winches

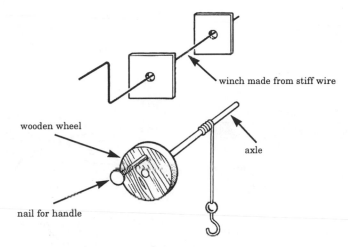

winch made from stiff wire

wooden wheel

axle

nail for handle

In some instances winches which carry a load must be prevented from winding backwards. A simple ratchet can be employed to achieve this. The ratchet consists of a toothed wheel and a bar which fits against the teeth to prevent movement in one direction only. Primary school children can easily make their own ratchets or use construction kits to achieve this effect.

Figure 3.12   A simple ratchet arrangement

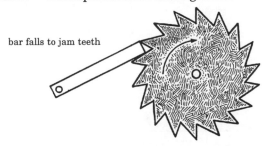

bar falls to jam teeth

the wheel turns clockwise but not anticlockwise

LEVERS, LINKAGES AND PIVOTS

A lever is a rigid shape which is able to turn around a pivot. The position of the pivot determines the type of lever and the effect obtained by moving it. A linkage is a rigid shape which connects levers and other moving parts and transmits movement from one part of a mechanism to another.

Figure 3.13 The three basic types of lever with everyday examples

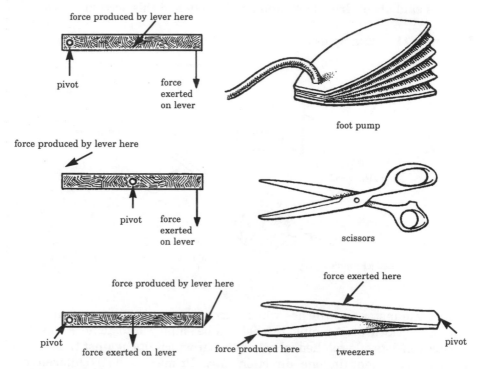

The dimensions of the lever will determine the forces required to move it and the forces produced by it.

Figure 3.14 Increasing and reducing forces with levers

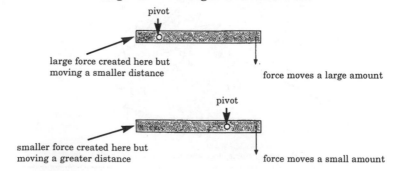

The main principles that primary school children might learn about levers are as follows:

LEVERS

- Levers are used in a wide variety of everyday devices.
- Levers can be of all shapes and sizes but must be made from rigid materials.
- Levers have a pivot point or fulcrum.
- Levers can transmit movement from one place to another.
- Linkages can be used with levers to transmit movements.
- Linkages can be rigid (card strips) or flexible (string).
- Linkages often require guide sleeves to work effectively.
- Levers can be returned to their original position by using a force provided by people, springs, elastic bands or gravity.
- The position of the pivot and dimensions of the lever have an effect on the type and distance of movement.
- The position of the pivot and dimensions of the lever have an effect on the forces used and produced.

Figure 3.15   Model monster showing many of the features mentioned.

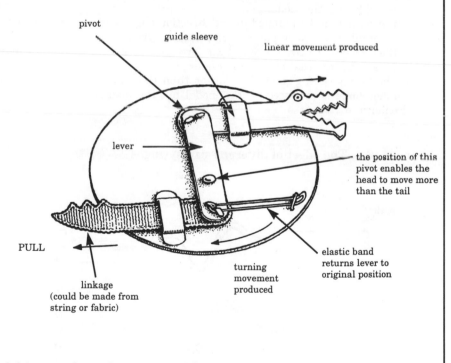

Model is seen from the reverse side.

PNEUMATICS AND HYDRAULICS

Pneumatics and hydraulics in the primary school involve the control of movement by transferring air or water along tubing. An increase of pressure at one end of the tube can result in a movement at the other end.

Control by pneumatics can be achieved by partially inflating a balloon or polythene bag with air using lungs, a squeezy bottle or a balloon pump or alternatively by using syringes. The control system becomes hydraulic if it is filled with water or other liquids. The devices are most often used in conjunction with levers, hinges and linkages.

The main principles that primary school children might learn about pneumatics and hydraulics are as follows:

PNEUMATICS AND HYDRAULICS

1   Air or water can be moved from one place to another along tubes.
2   Air and water can be moved by pushing them with various things such as flexible bottles, and syringes.
3   The moved air or water can move something at the end of the tubing such as a balloon, polythene bag or another syringe.
4   Levers and linkages can be set up to translate this movement into other kinds of movement.
5   Air is more easily squeezed than water and this will affect the control that is possible over the model.
6   Air or water can be pumped in one direction only by using a valve such as that found on a balloon pump or on a bicycle tyre.
7   If the two syringes are the same, the force on one and the distance it moves will be similar to that on the other one.
8   If the syringe being pushed is larger than the one on the model then a smaller force is produced on the model but the distance it moves will be greater and vice versa.

Figure 3.16   The effect of different size syringes

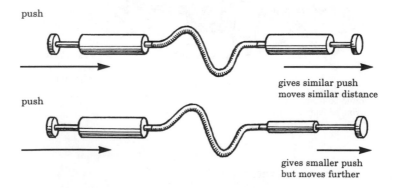

push

gives similar push
moves similar distance

push

gives smaller push
but moves further

Figure 3.17   A model controlled by squeezing a washing up bottle

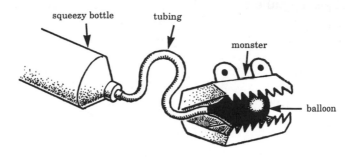

Figure 3.18   Model controlled by pushing or pulling a syringe

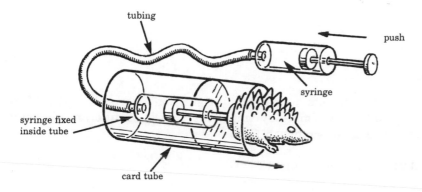

BELTS AND PULLEYS

The rotation of a wheel, a winch or an electric motor can be transferred elsewhere on a model by means of a drive belt on a set of pulleys. This simple system provides the opportunity to investigate gearing without the problems of using meshed gears. The drive belt can be a simple elastic band and the 'pulley' could simply be a cotton reel or the drive shaft itself as the following models show.

Figure 3.19   A set of models that children might build as part of their research into drive belts and pulleys

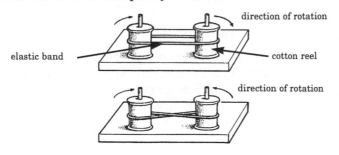

Figure 3.20   Model to show how a drive belt can be fixed on a drive shaft in place of a pulley

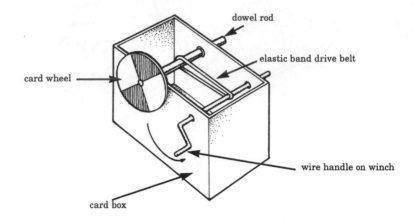

PULLEYS

Pulleys can be bought commercially to fit tightly on a variety of axles. They can also be made very simply by employing wheels of different diameter and making a suitable 'sandwich'.

Figure 3.21   Making a pulley

three wooden wheels

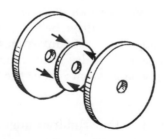

glue together as a sandwich

PULLEYS AND GEARING SYSTEMS

Two linked pulleys of the same diameter will rotate at the same speed but it is often more beneficial to slow down or speed up a rotation. A good example of this is when an electric motor is used in many models. Often the speed of the motor is much greater than is required in the model. In this instance different diameter pulleys can be used to turn a fast rotation into a slower one.

Figure 3.22 The effect of different size pulleys

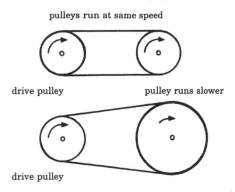

The diameter of a drive shaft can be varied by wrapping sticky tape around it so children can investigate gearing systems with simple equipment.

Figure 3.23 Example of a worksheet on drive belts and pulleys

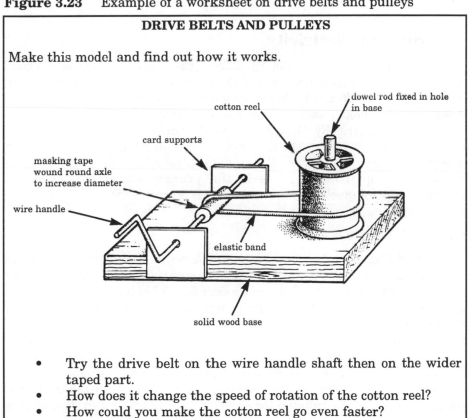

- Try the drive belt on the wire handle shaft then on the wider taped part.
- How does it change the speed of rotation of the cotton reel?
- How could you make the cotton reel go even faster?

The main principles that primary school children might learn about drive belts and pulleys are as follows:

DRIVE BELTS AND PULLEYS

- A pulley helps keep a drive belt in position and provides enough friction for it to move.
- A drive belt can transfer rotation from one shaft or axle to another.
- The correct drive belt tension is important in transferring movement successfully.
- The drive belt can be twisted to produce a reverse rotation. (See Figure 3.19).
- The drive belt can enable a vertical rotation to be turned into a horizontal rotation. (See Figure 3.23).
- A drive belt can drive more than one pulley at once.
- The relative diameter of the two pulleys will affect the speed of the driven pulley.
- Pulleys of the same diameter will run at the same speed of rotation.
- A small pulley driving a larger one will create a slower rotation and vice versa. (See Figure 3.22).

Control with Electricity

In the home, in industry and in many other places, there is a broad range of devices which are controlled by electricity or a combination of mechanisms and electricity. In the primary classroom components used in design and technology such as light bulbs, buzzers and electric motors can be controlled electrically. Designed products can be controlled through the use of a simple switch or set of switches some of which the children can design and make themselves. Electronic control of designed products can reach more sophisticated levels in the primary school by the use of computer control involving inputs as well as output devices.

Case Study – Doll's House

James and Catherine had been studying electrical circuits in their science lessons. They wanted to use some of the knowledge they had gained to make a model doll's house with a light and a door bell. They used a cardboard box with an open end and cut a large front door in the side with the help of their teacher. James decided to fix a bulb in a bulb holder from the 'ceiling' and run the wires outside to a battery. He made a lamp shade from coloured tissue paper for the light and operated it by touching the wire to the battery.

Meanwhile Catherine taped a buzzer to the inside of the box and arranged two wires into a push switch just by the side of the door. She completed a circuit by running the wires to a battery placed in the corner of the room. She spent considerable time devising a switch which would look attractive and work when pressed. She was keen that this switch was reliable and worked every time it was pressed. Later, James, who had noticed Catherine's door switch, asked her to help him make a wall switch for his light.

Case Study – Electric Vehicle

Aisha and Mikaela had made an electric powered buggy which carried the battery as well as the switch and motor. Their teacher asked them to find a way of turning off the motor when the vehicle hit against something such as a wall. The girls tried a number of ideas involving spring switches on the front of the vehicle. Eventually with some help from their teacher they devised a method which depended on something being thrown forward when the vehicle crashed. They placed a coin between two electrical contacts to complete the motor circuit. This would be displaced when the vehicle hit something.

Figure 3.24   Electric powered vehicle

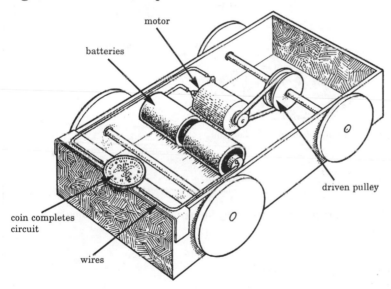

Electrical control by switches

Electrical switches can be operated in a variety of ways as the last example shows. They can operate when they are stepped on, tilted, pressed, turned or raised by water level. Children can design and make their own switches to operate in these different ways. The following technique will enable children to make their own components for a switch in the primary class-room. They can then go on to invent their own switches to meet their own requirements.

Figures 3.25 and 3.26 Making electrical switches

HOW TO MAKE YOUR OWN ELECTRICAL SWITCHES

- You can use aluminium foil to make connections and leads on a card base.
- Glue strips of the aluminium foil where you want them.

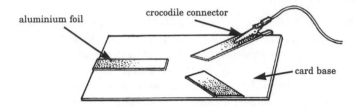

aluminium foil   crocodile connector   card base

- Make parts of your switch by covering card or plastic with aluminium foil.

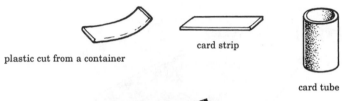

plastic cut from a container   card strip   card tube

wrap aluminium foil all around

- Make the part for your switch by shaping or punching holes in it with a hole punch

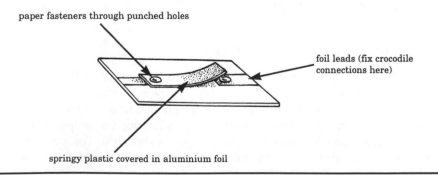

paper fasteners through punched holes

foil leads (fix crocodile connections here)

springy plastic covered in aluminium foil

The following information sheets show a variety of switches that children can make to incorporate in their models.

MAKING ELECTRICAL SWITCHES – 1

Figure 3.27   A turn switch

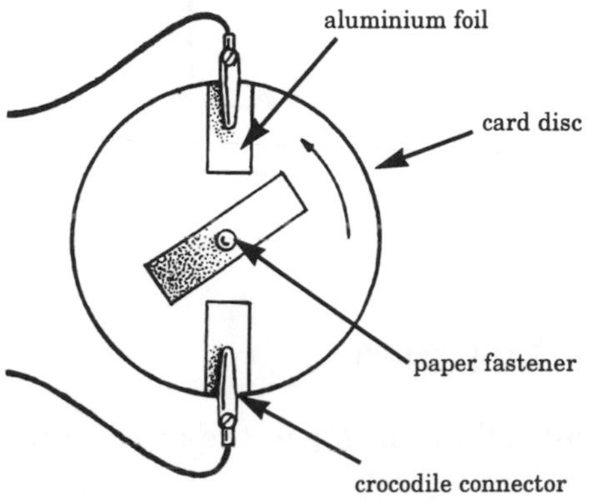

Figure 3.28   A pressure switch

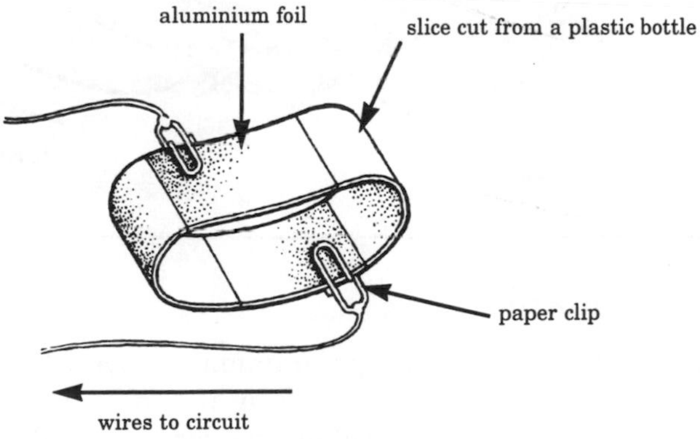

MAKING ELECTRICAL SWITCHES – 2

Figure 3.29   A turn switch

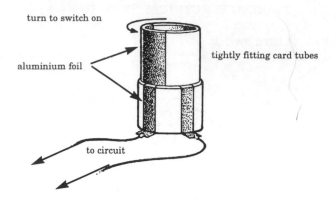

turn to switch on

aluminium foil

tightly fitting card tubes

to circuit

Figure 3.30   A tilt switch

The ball will roll down to join the aluminium foil contacts when the switch is tilted.

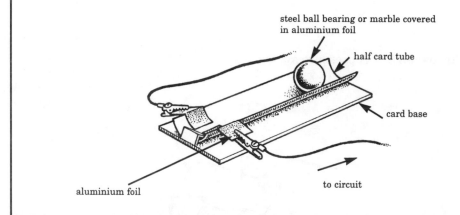

steel ball bearing or marble covered in aluminium foil

half card tube

card base

aluminium foil

to circuit

Programmable Toys

Many classrooms will have programmable toys which children can use to learn a great deal about control. Educational 'toys' such as Roamer, Pip or Big Track can be given a list of instructions either directly or in the form of a simple program or procedure. These devices provide an excellent introduction to the more sophisticated computer control as well as provide opportunities for children to develop mathematical, scientific and language concepts.

Computer Control

The products that children design and make in the primary school can be controlled by employing computers. The basic equipment needed will be a classroom computer together with an interface, some suitable software and a set of output components, such as bulbs, buzzers and motors, that can be built into models and then connected to the interface. Components which initiate various events, called input components, can be added at a later stage. These consist of simple switches, pressure pads, light sensitive switches or sensors, temperature sensors etc. Some educationalists would argue that both input and output devices should be introduced to children at the same time.

Children will benefit from having experience of the following before they exploit computer control to the full:

- using electrical circuits in models,
- designing and making the kind of models they might want to control;
- devising simple programs to control programmable toys or screen turtles.

Early experience in using electrical circuits will be gained in both science and design and technology lessons and the models which include electrical components can be as simple as a picture containing a light bulb. Much useful experience in devising programs of instructions can be developed through language work in the classroom. A child directing a blindfolded partner through a maze of desks and chairs in the classroom by giving clear instructions, is preparing for control technology. A child who learns to program an educational toy is learning how to give exact instructions in the correct sequence to achieve an end.

Some examples of design and make assignments using computer control include the following:

USING OUTPUT COMPONENTS ONLY:

- Design and make a greetings card in which there are one or two flashing lights.
- Design and make a card bust of a person which has a winking eye and whose bow-tie revolves sometimes.
- Design and make a model set of traffic lights which turn on and off in the correct sequence.
- Design and make a model fair ground ride with a rotating part and flashing coloured lights.

USING INPUT AND OUTPUT COMPONENTS:

- Design and make an alarm which is triggered by someone standing on a pressure pad.
- Design and make a level crossing barrier which lifts and whose lights flash when a toy vehicle approaches.
- Design something which would help a character in a well known story. For instance you might devise a way of helping Goldilocks escape when the three bears arrive.

3:   Structures and Forces

Introduction

An understanding of structures and the forces on them is fundamental to much of the work children do in primary design and technology. Structures are all around us. We cannot escape their influence but we may well take them for granted and therefore miss their significance. The chair you are sitting on is supported by certain structural principles which can be discussed and understood by primary aged children. The very same principles can be used in the construction of children's designed products.

The legs of the chair may be made of tubular material for lightness and strength and children will mirror this by making strong frameworks using art straws or card tubes. The chair may have a wooden frame which is secured with reinforced corner joints. Children in turn will make wood strip frameworks by gluing card corners at the joints. Many classroom chairs have moulded plastic seats which will have 'folds' at the edges to prevent excessive bending when sat upon. These folds can be employed when children use flat pieces of card which need to be made more rigid. The legs of many chairs are slightly spread out towards the floor to provide stability. An understanding of the forces involved will enable children to build models which use the principle of a broad base to prevent them falling over. Even the fabric covering on many chairs may possess a structure in its weave which provides strength at the same time as the essential flexibility.

Examples of products which employ structures are:

chairs and tables	bridges
egg boxes	buildings
vehicle chassis	camping tents
brick walls	play pens
clothing fabrics	packaging
counterpoise lamps	ball point pens
bicycles	motorcycle helmets

There are many examples in nature of successful supporting structures such as animal skeletons and plant stems.

Structures and the Forces on Them

Structures are affected by the forces on them:

- Forces can squash things, stretch things, twist things.
- Forces can hold things still or keep things moving with the same speed and direction.
- Forces can make things move faster, slow them down or change their direction.

Examples of things which provide forces are:

- Earth's gravity   always acts downwards towards the centre of the Earth;
- Friction   tries to oppose movement or potential movement;
- Buoyancy in water   on floating *and* sinking objects;
- Air resistance   especially on fast things like cars and rockets;
- Moving air or water   e.g. wind or water mills;
- Human muscles   provide a force which can be immediately measured by the provider;
- Magnets   attract other magnets and magnetic material (and also repel parts of other magnets);
- The floor   pushes up on whatever is standing on it.

STRUCTURES AND FORCES

Children should know that:

- All objects have a centre of gravity.
- Structures have different degrees of stability.
- Components of a structure can be strengthened.

> This can be achieved by:
> using more materials i.e. a thicker plank of wood
> shaping the material already in use ie by folding

- The whole structure can be strengthened by forming the components into:

> triangles;
> arches;
> or by using strong joints between components.

- Structures are subject to loading forces and internal forces:

> Forces acting from outside a structure will create a variety of forces inside the structure which may have to be resisted.

Centre of Gravity

The centre of gravity of something is where we can imagine the full force of gravity on that thing acts. Sometimes this is inside the thing or it can be outside in mid-air.

Figure 3.31   Person standing and a balancing parrot toy.

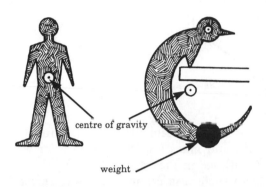

Stability

Free-standing models tend to fall over when their centre of gravity is allowed to move outside the outer limits of the base. This may happen if they are knocked or blown over or they are standing on a sloping surface.

Figure 3.32   Person standing on a slope. One is stable while the other is about to fall over

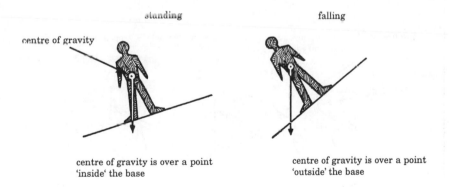

Models can be made more stable by:

1   Lowering the centre of gravity e.g. by providing more weight towards the base;
2   Providing a broader base.

Figure 3.33 Stable model traffic lights set in a weighted base and a broad base

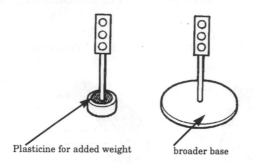

Plasticine for added weight   broader base

There are many ways to support free-standing models depending on their height, width and mass and the purpose for which they have been made. These are outlined in Part 4.

Some structures such as a crane or an Anglepoise lamp need to have a considerable part of their mass outside their base. In these cases a counterbalance may be required to maintain balance. In some cases a heavier base is used or an alternative would be to clamp the structure to a firm base such as the table top.

The following is an activity which can be adapted to help children understand the relationship between centre of gravity and stability.

Figure 3.34 How to find the centre of gravity of a piece of card

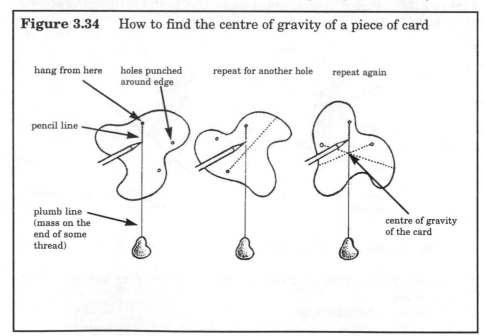

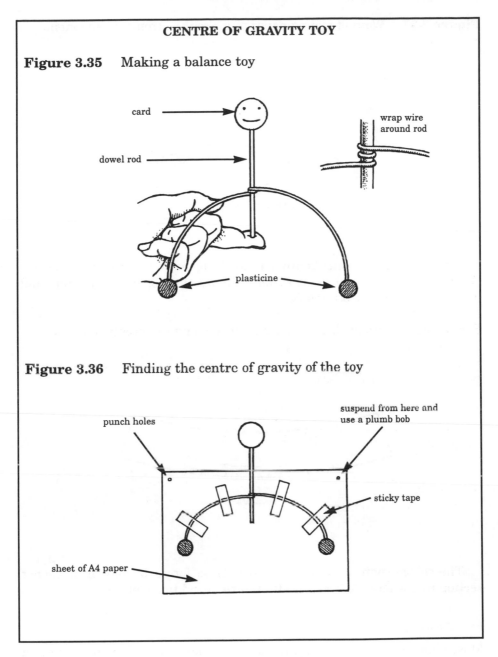

CENTRE OF GRAVITY TOY

Figure 3.35   Making a balance toy

card

wrap wire
around rod

dowel rod

plasticine

Figure 3.36   Finding the centre of gravity of the toy

punch holes

suspend from here and
use a plumb bob

sticky tape

sheet of A4 paper

Strength of the Components of a Structure

Parts of a structure can be strengthened by folding. A flat piece of paper becomes stronger if it is folded into a tube. A strip of card becomes more rigid if it is folded at right angles along its length. Corrugated card is stronger than the three flat pieces from which it is made.

113

Figure 3.37   Ways of folding paper to make it a stronger component

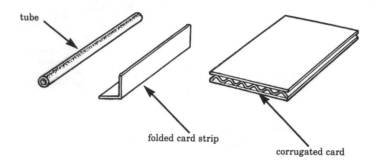

tube

folded card strip

corrugated card

These folded components are usually designed to resist bending forces. When a component is bent it suffers compression forces on one side and tension forces on the other side.

Figure 3.38   Simple beam showing tension and compression forces

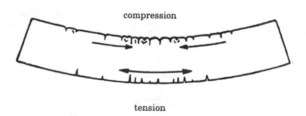

compression

tension

The folded material helps to resist these forces by having a deeper section just where the greatest effect of the bend takes place.

BUCKLING

Most folded components will fail due to buckling when they are subjected to bending forces. When the materials buckles it moves partially out of alignment at one point of weakness. Once this has begun, the buckle quickly becomes larger and failure becomes complete.

Figure 3.39   Examples of buckling in paper components

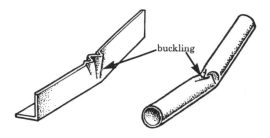

Strength of the Whole Structure

The whole structure can be arranged in such a way that the forces from the outside are resisted by a *spread* of forces inside.

TRIANGLES

A square or rectangular shape can easily fail at the corners and squash into a parallelogram. The corner joints here will bend into angles other than right angles. A triangular shape cannot fail at the corners because the angles cannot change. Failure can still occur in the sides of the triangle if these are stretched or compressed too much but this is less likely to happen than failure at the corners.

Figure 3.40   Rectangle collapsing under external load and triangle resisting load

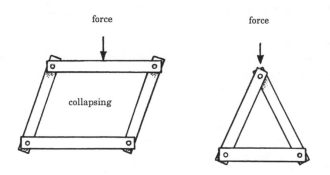

If corner joints are strengthened in a rectangular structure then the corner angles are more likely to remain at right angles and the rectangle will retain its shape. This is apparent in the wood strip/card corner method of construction.

ARCHES

An arch enables the forces within the structure to be transmitted to stronger parts of the structure, or to parts which are more readily supported i.e. at the base of the bridge or doorway.

Figure 3.41   Arch with internal forces shown

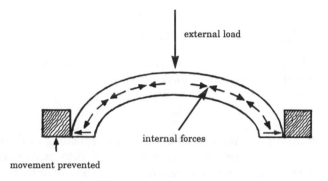

An egg shell or motorcycle crash helmet are good examples of the arch principle being used in a shell structure.

Loading Forces and Internal Forces

The external forces acting on a structure may be a result of:

- its own weight.
- the reaction of the surface upon which it stands, e.g. the river bank supports to a bridge.
- the weight of things it has to support eg the person sitting on a chair.
- something squeezing it, e.g. a hand using a pair of scissors.
- the wind, water or other things striking it.
- movement of the ground, e.g. in an earthquake.

These external forces will set up forces inside the structure. The forces may cause tension, compression, twisting or shearing within the components of the structure.

A piece of string will cope well with forces in tension but not in compression. A block of concrete will cope well with being compressed but not with tension forces. Appropriate materials must be chosen for different parts of a structure. For instance a tent pole slotted together will resist compression forces (but not tension forces) while the guy ropes have the opposite role.

Figure 3.42 Tent pole and guy ropes showing tension and compression forces

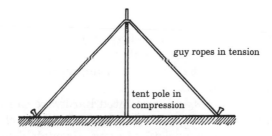

Figure 3.43 Compression and tension forces in the components of a simple truss girder bridge

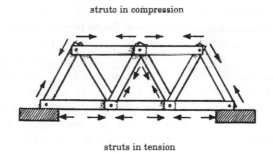

4: Information Technology, Products and Applications, Quality

Using Information Technology to Support Design and Technology

A knowledge of information technology (IT) can be of benefit in carrying out design and make assignments but it is not essential. IT should be seen as a tool which should be used, when appropriate, to enhance children's learning within the subject.

The use of computers and associated hardware can be likened to using a pair of scissors. Teachers would expect to show children how to use scissors effectively in a variety of ways through direct instruction and demonstration. We would expect scissors to be used, when appropriate, in all curriculum areas. We would not, however, provide separate lessons in the use of scissors without providing a meaningful context. In the same way we would expect IT to be chosen as a tool by children in all curriculum subjects once they had been introduced to its potential. IT is a much more complex and sophisticated tool than a pair of scissors, however, and its true potential is constantly being revealed and exploited. There is no logical link, however, between IT and design and technology any more than there is between IT and maths or science or English.

Some confusion may have been generated by the inclusion of IT in the first National Curriculum document for design and technology (DES, 1990). For some teachers this marriage of convenience has distorted the true character of design and technology, giving it an unwarranted 'high-tech' image. Things are becoming clearer now that there are separate documents for IT and design and technology and in some initial teacher education institutions separate courses are being developed for IT.

Information technology can be conveniently described in terms of a set of applications which are appropriate for supporting work in primary school design and technology such as:

- word-processing
- desktop publishing
- art and graphic packages including computer aided design (CAD)
- music and sound packages

- databases
- spreadsheets
- computer control technology, including programmable toys
- simulations
- Datalogging
- CD-ROM
- context specific, computer aided learning packages.

The following examples of design and make tasks illustrate how these IT applications can be used to support and enhance work in design and technology.

DESIGN THE INSIDE OF A NEW BEDROOM – ART & GRAPHICS

Children make a model of the interior of a new bedroom in a cardboard box. They consider new furniture, artificial lighting, carpeting, curtains and bedspread. The children use a computer art and graphics package to design a range of new wallpapers to choose from.

The children begin by lining the box for their model bedroom with suitable carpet, wallpaper and curtains for the window. Off-cuts of real carpet and fabrics can be used. The wallpaper is designed to match, using a variety of possibilities printed from a computer art package. The art package will permit the children to create an image and repeat this over and over again and also to turn it upside down or make a reflection. Different colours can be tried on screen before printing out the wall paper and lining the walls of the bedroom with it.

ILLUSTRATE A SHORT STORY OR A POEM USING SHADOW PUPPETS – WORD-PROCESSING, TAPE RECORDER, CONTROL TECHNOLOGY

Children take a short story or a poem (for instance an Aesop's fable or a poem from Prefabulous Animiles by James Reeves) and illustrate this with shadow puppets. They use a wordprocessor to write their own script, a tape recorder to record sound effects and control technology to produce 'stage effects' such as flashing lighting.

The shadow puppet screen can be made by stretching greaseproof paper or muslin across the legs of an upturned chair or desk. Shadow puppets can be made from card and if necessary jointed. These can be held with wire or wooden rods.

Children write the script for a narrator using a wordprocessor enabling redrafting as ideas develop. Sound effects can be made with musical instruments or other common items and recorded on a tape recorder if appropriate. Computer control technology can be used to trigger certain 'stage effects' such as alarm buzzers, flashing lights or scenery moved by electric motor.

MAKE A MODEL CAGE FOR A SMALL PET – CD-ROM, DATABASES

Children choose a small pet such as a hamster or gerbil and use a computer database or information on a CD-ROM to find out what it requires to live comfortably in a cage. They use this information to design and make a model of the cage to show a potential manufacturer. Pets such as hamster, gerbil, mouse, rat, guinea pig, rabbit, tortoise, goldfish and budgie could be chosen. Features such as cage size and eating requirements should be established before the design proceeds.

DESIGN AND MAKE A PERSONALITY BADGE – ART & GRAPHICS PACKAGE

Children design and make a badge which shows something of the character as well as the name of the owner. They decide the occasion upon which it is worn. The badge must resemble a commercially produced one and be designed and printed using a computer art package. Children devise their own method for fixing the badge to its owner such as safety pin, paper clip, Velcro, clothes peg etc.

The design for the badge is developed on a computer art and graphics package. A number of ideas are produced and printed before choosing the best one. The children use the draw and paint facilities together with colour and text to develop their badge design. Badges can be printed out in colour or in black and white and coloured with felt pens.

PLAN THE FOOD FOR A PARTY – SPREADSHEET

Children plan and make the food for a party at school. They use a computer spreadsheet to record the ingredients required and how much these will cost. The spreadsheet can be altered to take account of different numbers of guests or the varying prices of the ingredients.

Figure 3.44   Example spreadsheet – Number of guests: 28

Ingredient	number of items required	cost of one at Safebury's (pence)	total cost Safebury's (pence)	cost of one at Tessway (pence)	total cost Tessway (pence)
packet crisps	28	25	700	24	672
peanuts–500g	14	90	1260	88	1232
box fancy cakes	1	68	68	75	75
bread rolls	56	9	504	10	560
1/2 dozen eggs	4	82	328	82	328
pkt sausages	2	124	248	120	240
carrots–500g	4	25	100	24	96
pkt biscuits	4	48	192	50	200
carton cress	6	29	174	24	144
butter–250g	2	53	106	48	96
TOTAL			3680		3643

The party food might be for a picnic in summer or an end-of-term celebration. Children look at a variety of recipes for party food and use these ideas to create their own dishes. The food might involve uncooked arrangements of vegetables, packet snacks or spreads. Alternatively there may be facilities for cooking small sausages, eggs, pizzas, or biscuits etc.

Children draw up a list of ingredients and quantities required. The computer spreadsheet is set up to calculate the cost of each ingredient for a given number of guests. Different costing may be entered to take account of using different shops.

MAKE A COMMERCIAL FOR TELEVISION – MUSIC PACKAGE, ART & GRAPHICS

Children plan and carry out a television commercial for a real or imaginary product. They use a computer music package to make a suitable jingle and prepare any still pictures using a graphics package. They plan their presentation using a cartoon strip technique which shows the development of their advertisement. Children choose a suitable product which may be one they have made themselves. Their commercial will only last a few seconds but they must plan it in detail. The children use a card frame as a television screen in which to carry out their performance.

DESIGN SOME REFLECTIVE CLOTHING – DATALOGGING

Children design and make an article which could be worn by a cyclist or a lollipop person to enable others to see them in poor light conditions. They use computer Datalogging equipment to find out which materials reflect light the best and use this information to support their designs.

The children interview someone who needs to be seen in poor light conditions – for instance a policeman, a jogger or a school child. Once they understand the need to use reflective materials they carry out their research by using a light sensor with data logging equipment in a variety of light conditions. They test materials such as aluminium foil, white cotton, fluorescent fabrics, sequinned material, plastics and so on.

Another way to be seen in poor light is to use something which moves. Children combine these ideas to make a device which is full size or to scale.

DESIGN AN INTERACTIVE SCIENCE DISPLAY – DESKTOP PUBLISHING, WORD-PROCESSING

A group of children make a 'hands-on' display which demonstrates some simple scientific ideas such as electric circuits, magnetism or reflection in two mirrors. The display is accompanied by some attractive posters which explain what to do and how things work. These are produced with the help of a computer desk-top publishing package.

The children take a science idea or statement such as 'A short pendulum swings at a different speed to a longer one' and set up a display to demonstrate this. They develop a simple set of instructions using a wordprocessor to go with their display and evaluate these by testing them on their friends. The instructions are then redrafted in the light of this evaluation. The children evaluate the whole display by writing a short questionnaire for their audience.

There are many more examples of effective and appropriate use of IT to support design and technology but these few serve to illustrate the possibilities.

Products and Applications

A knowledge of the products and applications which have been designed and made by others has two major functions in the education of primary aged children:

1   It will increase the children's repertoire of skills, knowledge and understanding which will enable them to design and make their own products.
2   It will promote an increased understanding and critical awareness of the designed world in which children live and in which they are increasingly the consumer.

Both of these functions will involve a consideration of:

- the needs of the person(s) for whom the product was made (the client(s));
- the purpose of the product;
- its fitness for purpose;
- the value judgements made when designing and making the product;
- the value judgements made when using the product;
- how well the product was designed;
- how well the product was made.

The evaluation of others' products in order to support children's own designing and making has been dealt with at length in Part 2. Here it was argued that this kind of evaluation might occur during the following parts of children's design procedures:

- investigating the context for designing and making;
- identifying needs and opportunities and clarifying the design and make task;
- evaluating products and processes in design and technology;
- researching the task and its possible solutions.

In looking at the designed products of others, children become aware of the many requirements demanded of them within their own designing and making. An identification of the specifications a designer might have made in designing a pull-along toy for a four-year-old will encourage the pupil to be clear about his or her own specifications for a designed product made in the classroom. A research task in which children make critical judgements about a collection of different desk tidies will provide useful data regarding the child's own design for such a device.

Children's Awareness of the Designed World

Sometimes the emphasis in evaluating others' designed products will be more on gaining an awareness of the designed world rather than as having a direct impact on a child's own design and make task. This will often be the case when products are evaluated as a part of the work in other curriculum areas. Children may evaluate kitchen utensils from the World War II era as part of their history project or dwellings from different countries as part of geography. There may be no intention that they design and make kitchen utensils or model houses themselves.

In these instances the generic skills and knowledge and understanding that children gain can be thought of as having an indirect effect on any designing and making the child does in the future. Whatever the circumstances, a knowledge of 'the technical, economic, aesthetic, environmental and moral criteria' (DfEE, 1996) used in designing and making products will form an important part of any child's education.

The value judgements made when others design and make products and consumers buy and use these, can often be made explicit through discussion and questioning in the primary classroom. Children can then be made aware that they too will make similar judgements when they design and make.

Making Value Judgements When Children Design and Make

In the classroom, *technical* judgements are made when children decide which mechanism will give the required movement and how they might achieve a particular flavour in a soup they are making. *Economics* will be considered when children consider how to cut a shape from a sheet of card without undue wastage. Teachers will be keen to emphasize economical use of materials, space and time. Children will be encouraged to consider the *aesthetic* aspects of their emerging products by considering things like the appearance, feel, taste and the appropriateness for its setting of certain products.

The *environmental* impact of a product will involve a consideration of the use of materials appropriate to the setting in which the product will be used and the environmental impact of using certain materials. Pollution effects and the use of recycled materials might be considered. Children might consider the effect of making their design for a playground seat in plastics rather than other materials which might fit in better with the surroundings. They might discuss the environmental impact of using tropical hardwoods to create furniture for the classroom.

Some design and make projects will enable children to consider wider *moral* issues such as when they design and make devices associated with war (the mangonel, fort or model rocket) or for disabled people.

Identifying Value Judgements in Others' Designed Products

The following questions might be asked by the primary teacher to encourage the identification of the value judgements which might have influenced the design and use of products:

FIRST IMPRESSIONS

What is the first thing that comes into your head about this product?

- What good feelings does it give you?
- What bad feelings does it give?
- Would you like to own it?

MAKING THE PRODUCT

- Why was it made?
- Are the best materials used to make the product?
- Can you think of more appropriate ones?
- What things that you cannot see now, were used to make the product? (Think of tools, workforce and energy sources used).
- Do you think making it had an effect on the environment or the people who made it?
- Could the product have been made in a better way?

OBTAINING AND VALUING THE PRODUCT

- Do you think it is easy to get something like this product?
- How much money do you think it would cost?
- Who do you think it would be worth a lot to?
- Who would it not be worth much to?

USING THE PRODUCT

- Who will use the product?

- Will it affect anyone besides the person who uses it?
- Will it have an effect on the environment when it is used?
- How will it change the person who uses it?
- Is it built to last or will it be thrown away quickly?
- Where will it finally end up when its use is over?

Quality, Safety and Vocabulary

QUALITY OF THE DESIGNED PRODUCT

The issue of quality in design and technology is closely related to the concepts of evaluation of processes and products and fitness for purpose. Children should be encouraged to consider the following in relation to the products they and others design and make:

1   How well was the product *designed* and how well it was *made*?
2   How well does the product fit the purpose for which it was made?

Children should become aware that products can be badly designed and yet well made. For instance a beautifully hand-crafted toilet roll holder may be too narrow to take the largest roll. A toy for a three-year-old may be fun to play with, attractive and well constructed and yet contain small components which come loose and might be swallowed.

Equally, some products might be well designed and yet badly made such as an attractive ball point pen with rough edges making it uncomfortable to hold. A model made by a child which falls apart because not enough glue was used fits into this category.

Fitness for purpose has been discussed in Part 2. It involves being clear about the purpose of the product in the first instance, by being clear about the specifications for the product. Once this has been established the fitness can be evaluated by a variety of means outlined in Part 2.

HEALTH AND SAFETY

Children will need to consider two major aspects of their work in design and technology with regards to health and safety.

- Health and safety issues while they are designing and making.
- Health and safety issues regarding the use of designed products (both their own and those of others).

Many health and safety issues that arise in design and technology in the classroom are the same as those for other curriculum subjects such as science and art and craft. Teachers will want to make their children aware of the potential for accidents and to discuss how these might be avoided before they happen. Children will be made aware of the potential for harming others in the classroom as well as themselves.

Children consider the safety of the products they make as part of their drawing up specifications for their products. Some of these specifications will only become apparent as work proceeds such as when a health hazard presents itself for the first time. Children should increasingly be able to predict potential hazards as their experience grows.

USE OF APPROPRIATE VOCABULARY

Teachers constantly handle the issue of teaching appropriate vocabulary in all curriculum subjects. Design and technology is no different. The most effective way to encourage children to use the correct vocabulary is first for the teacher to be familiar with the recommended vocabulary and then second for this to be progressively introduced into discussions with children. The Design and Technology Association publish a booklet of recommended vocabulary for use in primary schools (DATA, 1995b).

Part Four

Practical Capability in Design and Technology

Introduction

Practical capability in design and technology can be represented by the third level in the pupil's toolbox of skills and knowledge (page 21). It is a new concept which, as yet, has not been fully explored and therefore this Part represents the first stages in a longer term debate on the subject. Practical capability constitutes an aspect of design and technology which is not found in other curriculum subjects and therefore it is the ingredient which makes the subject unique. One might claim that *designing and making skills* can be employed in other subjects such as science, mathematics, English and art, and that much of the *knowledge and understanding* associated with the subject is 'borrowed' from the science and arts curricula. *Practical capability*, however, belongs to design and technology.

Practical capability is the ability to cope with practical situations and problems. It is about possessing a repertoire of knowledge, skills and abilities and combining these with a degree of inventiveness and adaptability. The practically capable person will handle familiar practical situations with ease and tackle new practical challenges with confidence.

Some adults and possibly even children will claim that they are not 'practically minded'. Some will say that they are 'all fingers and thumbs' when it comes to doing certain practical things. While many people will readily pick up a screw driver and change the fuse in a plug, others will prefer to leave such jobs to someone else. Many adults enjoy creating food dishes by using recipes of their own while a few avoid such creative pursuits. To believe one is not practically capable is akin to believing one cannot draw. It is a false belief which primary school teachers cannot afford to entertain. Without a degree of practical capability, teachers cannot teach design and technology. The good news is that teachers can gain the necessary practical capability in a number of ways as long as they believe they can.

Everyone has some practical capability within them. If they have enjoyed making their own clothes, putting up shelves, gardening, or creative cookery then they will already have an ability in a practical sense. Those who played with construction kits, created dens in the garden, made scale models or built sand castles when they were younger already have gained some practical capability. In school, the teacher gains practical capability by mounting wall displays, creating props for a school play or preparing materials for a reception class craft lesson.

In design and technology it is the teacher, initially, who needs a practical capability so that when children come to her with problems she will have some idea in her mind how these might be solved. She will not necessarily *tell* the child how to solve the problem but will be able to lead the child in the right direction. If a child is having problems with the wheels jamming on a model vehicle then the teacher has to be able to see what is going wrong and guide the child towards using spacers or a different wheel and axle arrangement.

Adapting Practical Techniques

Practical capability is partly about adapting practical techniques to new situations. For instance a child might be taught how to fix art straws together by using short lengths of pipe cleaner. This enables the child to make simple geometric three dimensional shapes using an art straw frame. The child might subsequently be asked to design and make an unusual jewellery box by covering an artstraw frame with paper 'cladding'. Later, the child might *choose* to use this ability to make a framework in a completely new situation such as in designing and making a Christmas tree decoration. In this assignment the child might be given a free choice as to how to create the decoration and will draw upon an increasing set of ideas, such as the art straw technique, for making the kind of product that is wanted.

In another situation a child might learn how to score and fold card effectively. The knowledge that thick material can be compressed or cut half way through in order to obtain a clean fold will be stored away for future use. When, in another design and make assignment, the child needs to fold a corrugated plastic sheet then this previous knowledge might be drawn upon together with some of the practical skill already gained. This will enable the child to make a half way cut into the corrugated sheet with a sharp knife and metal safety rule in order to achieve a clean fold.

Areas of Practical Capability

It is possible to identify broad areas of practical capability within which children might gain experience throughout their time in the primary school:

- Basic construction – marking, cutting and shaping materials.
- Basic construction – joining and fixing materials and components.
- Making things stand up in a stable way.
- Enabling parts of a product to turn.
- Making hinges, pivots and fulcrums.
- Creating strong frameworks – shell frames, strut frames, sheet frames.
- Employing finishing techniques.
- Making wheeled vehicles.
- Harnessing sources of energy for driving models.
- Using textiles in construction.
- Controlling movement.

Within each area there are manipulative skills and 'tricks of the trade' to bo learnt that can be employed when the right moment arrives. The list outlined above can provide a useful checklist for schools who have developed their scheme of work for design and technology. This would enable them to ensure that children receive a balance of practical capability skills while in the primary school.

The remainder of this Part sets out a vocabulary of basic practical ideas to support the teacher. The pages might provide ideas for practical workshop sessions which could be carried out during in-service work for teachers. They illustrate the potential for such work rather than set out a comprehensive programme. In addition, each page of ideas might be used as a quick reference for teachers in the classroom as they help children to solve problems. Some of the ideas can be adapted by the teacher to form focused practical tasks which might support children's design and make tasks.

Basic Construction Techniques – Marking, Cutting and Shaping Materials

Marking, cutting and shaping a wide variety of materials requires a range of practical skills. The practically capable child will know which tool is most appropriate to use with a particular material and be able to suggest alternatives if problems arise. For instance, when cutting a plastic lemonade bottle in half is it best to use a saw, a sharp knife or a pair of scissors? How will the bottle be secured in a safe manner when it is being cut? Previous experience might suggest supporting the bottle (with its top on to keep it 'blown up') in a vice while an initial slit is made with a sharp knife. A pair of scissors can then be used by inserting the point into this slit and cutting around a neat circle.

A key safety feature when cutting resistant materials is to hold the material in a secure manner, with fingers well clear of any cutting tools. In the case of wood or some plastics the material can be held on a bench hook or secured in a vice or with a G clamp.

Figure 4.1   Cutting with a sharp knife and safety rule

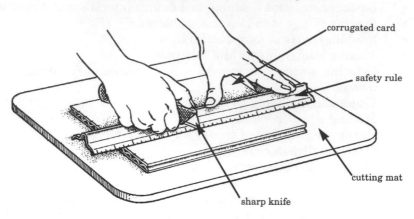

corrugated card

safety rule

cutting mat

sharp knife

Figure 4.2   Cutting with a junior hacksaw

push the wood and bench hook securely
against the table or bench

bench hook

bench hook block

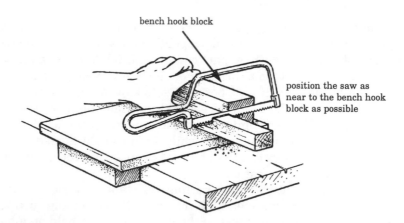

position the saw as
near to the bench hook
block as possible

Figure 4.3 Drilling holes

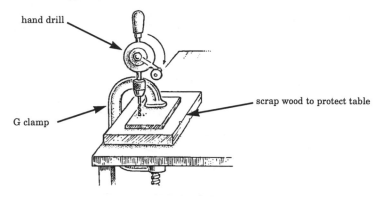

hand drill

scrap wood to protect table

G clamp

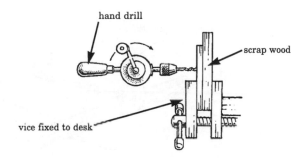

hand drill

scrap wood

vice fixed to desk

Figure 4.4 Cutting food products

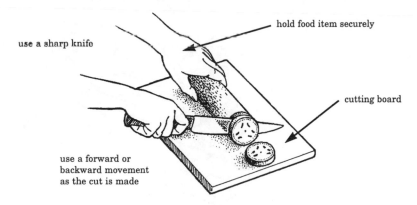

hold food item securely

use a sharp knife

cutting board

use a forward or
backward movement
as the cut is made

Figure 4.5   Scoring card

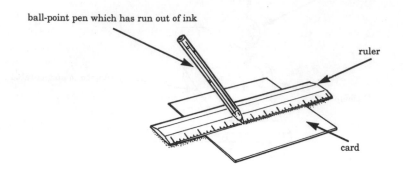

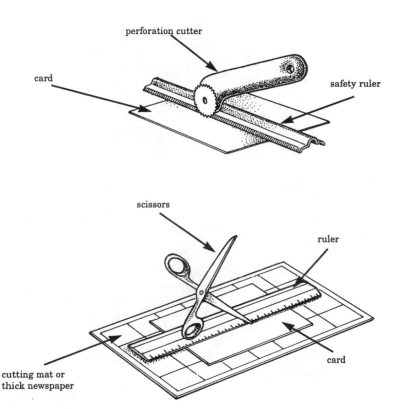

Basic Construction Techniques – Joining and Fixing Materials and Components

A wide range of materials will require joining together when children design and make their products. This can be done in a variety of ways, some of which are illustrated below. It is an advantage sometimes to have parts of a model joined in semi-permanent ways so that these can be taken apart when modifications to the model are made. For instance it is a good idea to have tightly fitting wheels which can, if necessary, be removed from an axle rather than have these permanently fixed with glue. Some materials such as metals (drinks cans and wire) require specialist adhesives to fix them. In the primary classroom a hot glue gun might be used or less attractive alternatives such as sticky tape might be employed.

Figure 4.6   Ways of joining paper and card

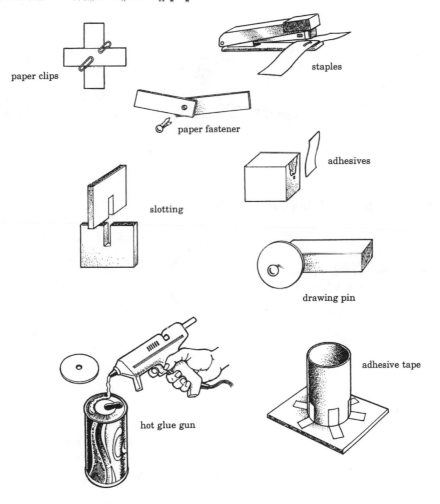

133

Figure 4.7   Ways of joining wood strips

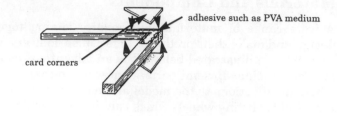

adhesive such as PVA medium

card corners

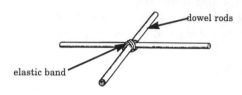

dowel rods

elastic band

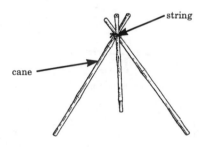

string

cane

Figure 4.8   Joining wire by twisting etc.

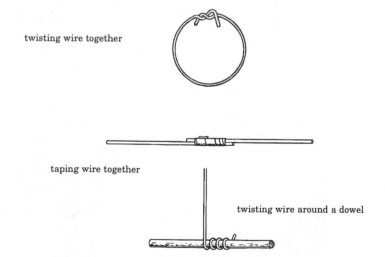

twisting wire together

taping wire together

twisting wire around a dowel

Making Things Stand Up in a Stable Way

The subject of the stability of free standing models was explored in Part 3. A model will stand in a stable fashion if it has a wide base or its centre of gravity is relatively low down. The presence of both of these conditions will ensure even more stability. The following types of product may need a degree of stability:

- a model windmill made to test the strength of the wind;
- a model desk lamp;
- a model crane;
- a cardboard cut out shape which needs to stand up;
- a tower which has to support a weight;
- a support for an aerial ropeway.

Some ideas for achieving stability in a model are illustrated below.

Figure 4.9(a) Ways of making a model stand up

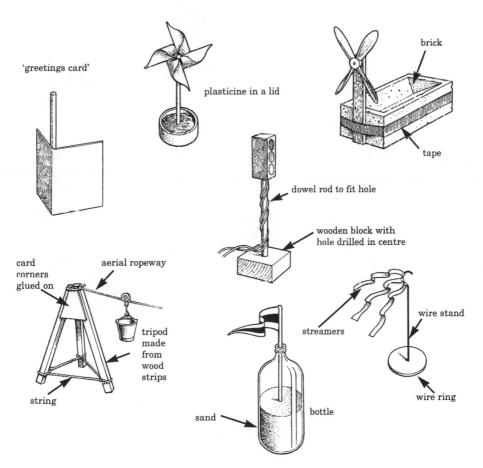

Figure 4.9(b) Ways of making a model stand up

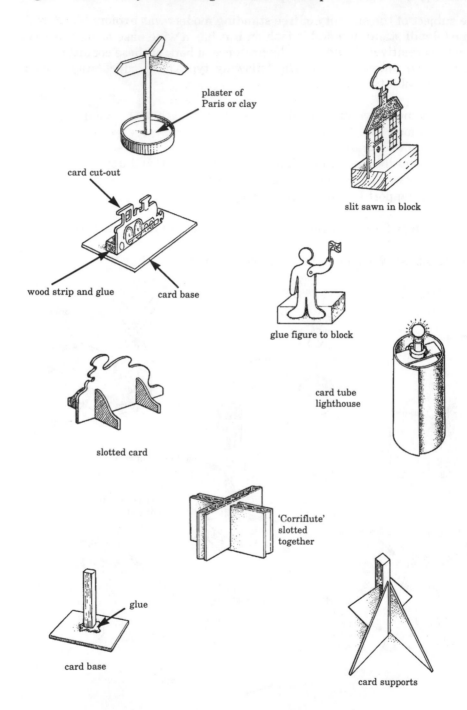

plaster of
Paris or clay

card cut-out

slit sawn in block

wood strip and glue

card base

glue figure to block

slotted card

card tube
lighthouse

'Corriflute'
slotted
together

glue

card base

card supports

Enabling Parts of a Product to Turn

For parts of a model to turn effectively the following conditions must be met:

- the part should be supported on an axle or spindle;
- the axle or spindle may turn or be fixed;
- friction between moving parts must be kept to a minimum.

The following types of product might require rotating parts:

- a model clock face;
- a greetings card with a moving part;
- a model crane;
- a wheeled vehicle;
- a model windmill;
- a model merry-go-round;
- a model driven by a propeller.

Wheels, axles, winches and handles are discussed on pages 91–5. Some ideas for achieving smoothly rotating parts in products are illustrated below.

Figure 4.10   Propeller and bead arrangement

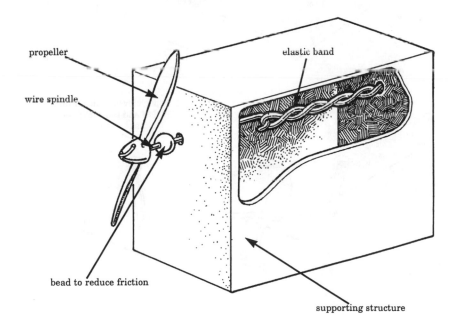

propeller

elastic band

wire spindle

bead to reduce friction

supporting structure

Figure 4.11   Spindle supported in two places

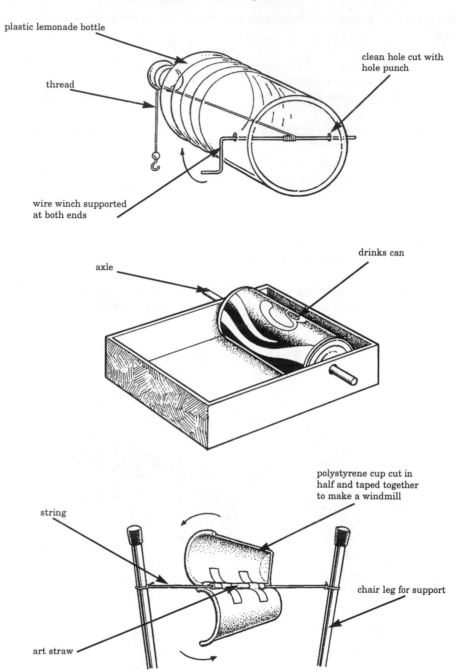

Figure 4.12   Spindle supported at one end only

A spindle supported at one end only, must be held **firmly**.

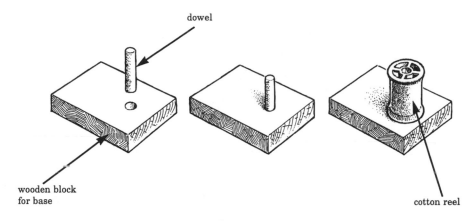

Alternative spindles fixed at one end

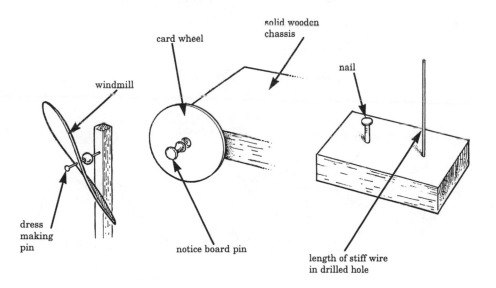

Figure 4.13   Using drive belts

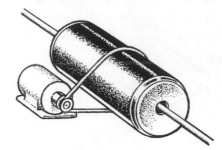

use a drinks can as a pulley **and** wheel

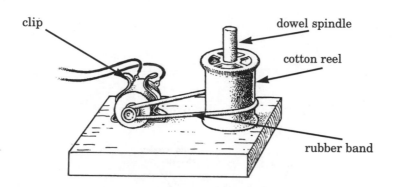

clip

dowel spindle

cotton reel

rubber band

fix a merry-go-round to the cotton reel

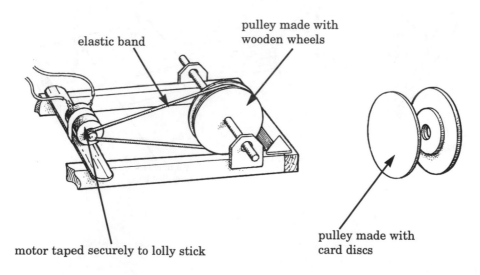

elastic band

pulley made with
wooden wheels

motor taped securely to lolly stick

pulley made with
card discs

Making Hinges, Pivots and Fulcrums

Pivots and fulcrums are discussed on pages 96–7. These are all devices for allowing a partial rotation of a lever or component.

Hinges might be used in:

- a model doll's house for the door;
- a model castle's drawbridge;
- a model vehicle door;
- a trap door on a model stage set.

Pivots and fulcrums are used in:

- all types of lever mechanisms;
- jointed puppets;
- a model see-saw;
- at the end of a control rod for a mechanical hand;
- in pop-up card engineering.

There are many different ways of producing a hinge or a pivot. Some of these are illustrated below.

Figure 4.14   Ways of making a hinge

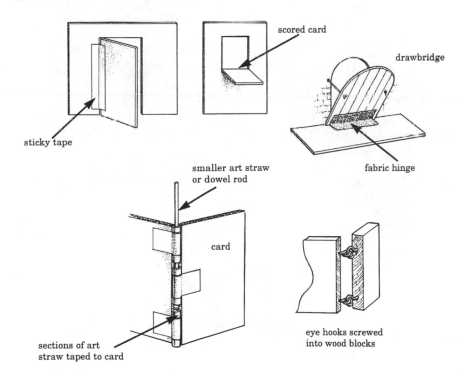

Figure 4.15   Ways of making moving joints

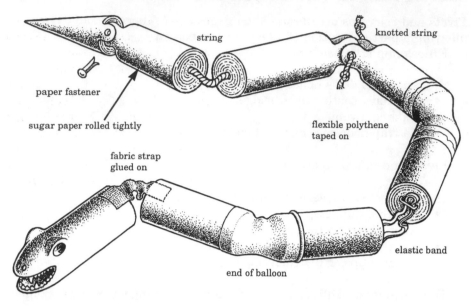

Figure 4.16   Ways of making pivots

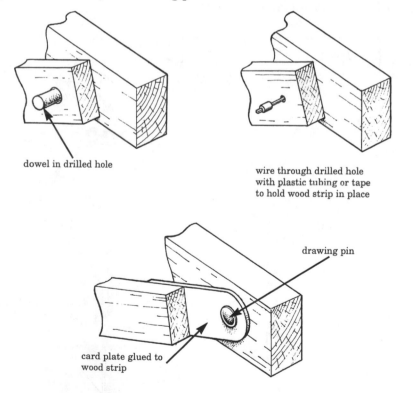

Creating Strong Frameworks

Many designed products found in everyday life are built upon a strong frame which may or may not be exposed. A settee is sometimes built around a frame which is never seen while a deck chair is a clear example of an exposed framework. Frameworks can be divided into strut frames, shell frames and sheet frames. A strut frame is generally made by joining strips of materials such as wood together to form cuboids or similar 3D shapes. Shell frames gain their strength from the shape of the shell in the same way that an egg or a crash helmet does. These might be made out of papier mâché or mouldable plastic foam such as Formafoam. A sheet frame is made from sheets of material such as in a card box or tube. Childrens' models will often require a strong frame as a basis for building upon. Strong frameworks might be used in the construction of:

- a vehicle chassis;
- a model bridge;
- a model building such as a doll's house;
- a box;
- an irregular shape like a mask, built on a chicken wire frame;
- the body and head of a puppet.

Some techniques for making strong frameworks are shown below.

Figure 4.17(a)   Making strong frameworks

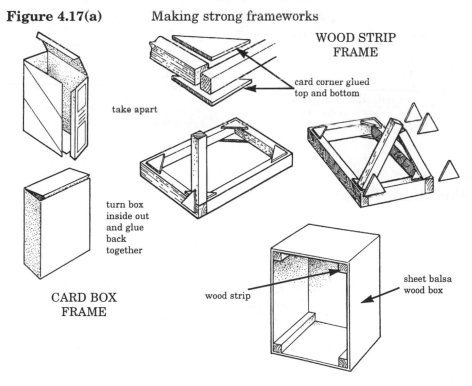

WOOD STRIP FRAME

card corner glued top and bottom

take apart

turn box inside out and glue back together

CARD BOX FRAME

wood strip

sheet balsa wood box

Figure 4.17(b)   Making strong frameworks

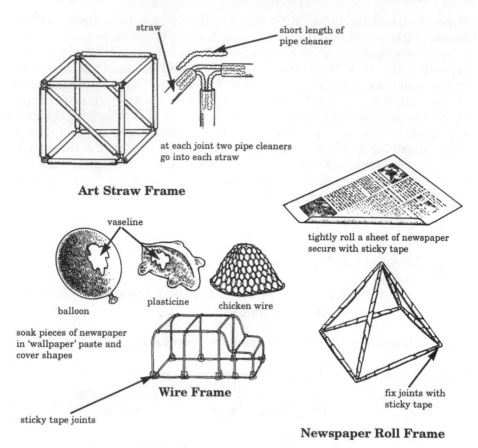

straw

short length of
pipe cleaner

at each joint two pipe cleaners
go into each straw

Art Straw Frame

vaseline

balloon

plasticine

chicken wire

tightly roll a sheet of newspaper
secure with sticky tape

soak pieces of newspaper
in 'wallpaper' paste and
cover shapes

Wire Frame

sticky tape joints

fix joints with
sticky tape

Newspaper Roll Frame

**Shell Frameworks from
Papier mâché**

Finishing Techniques

Finishing is to do with the final appearance of a product or its smooth
functioning. This might include adding a covering or cladding, using paint,
smoothing a surface with glasspaper or adding some form of decoration
such as sequins or glacé cherries.

A broad definition of cladding might include any method for covering the
structure of a model or filling in spaces in it with a relatively thin panel.
Examples of this might include:

- covering the chassis and framework of a model vehicle with card to make it look more realistic;
- covering a cuboid framework of wood strips to enclose the space to form a box;
- covering a chicken wire frame with papier mâché to form a dome shape for a hat;
- covering a card tube with fabric to form a puppet body.

Figure 4.18 Using cladding to finish a model

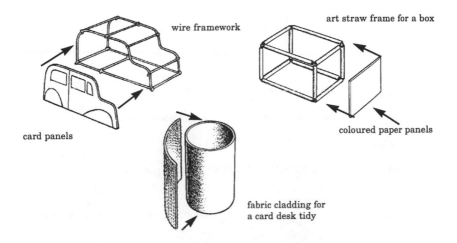

wire framework

art straw frame for a box

card panels

coloured paper panels

fabric cladding for a card desk tidy

The cladding itself may require further finishing. Examples of finishing techniques are shown below.

Figure 4.19 Add lettering and other graphic designs

Stencilling

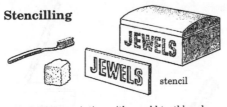

JEWELS

JEWELS stencil

use spatter painting with an old toothbrush or dab paint on with a sponge

paste computer generated designs onto a package

Figure 4.20   Sticky tape designs on a plastic apron

use sticky tape to make designs on a plastic apron

Figure 4.21   Smoothing and colouring techniques

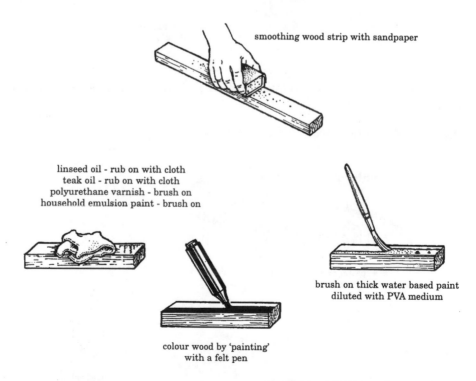

smoothing wood strip with sandpaper

linseed oil - rub on with cloth
teak oil - rub on with cloth
polyurethane varnish - brush on
household emulsion paint - brush on

brush on thick water based paint
diluted with PVA medium

colour wood by 'painting'
with a felt pen

Finishing Treatments for Wood

146

Making Wheeled Vehicles

Wheels and axles have been discussed as mechanisms on pages 91–4. Wheeled vehicles have two basic elements:

(1)   the chassis; and
(2)   the wheel and axle assembly.

In addition to these two elements, some wheeled vehicles have an in-board source of power such as an electric motor or a balloon. A vehicle may also have some form of body work to cover all or parts of it.

The chassis on all wheeled vehicles must be rigid but can be made from a wide variety of materials and components.

Figure 4.22   Different ways to make a chassis

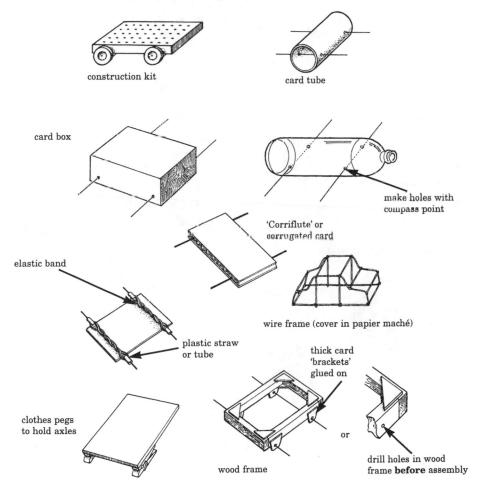

Vehicle chassis should be rigid and have clean holes for the axles

construction kit

card tube

card box

make holes with compass point

'Corriflute' or corrugated card

elastic band

wire frame (cover in papier maché)

plastic straw or tube

thick card 'brackets' glued on

clothes pegs to hold axles

wood frame

or

drill holes in wood frame **before** assembly

Wheels and axles can be made from a wide range of materials and components

Figure 4.23   Wheels and axles

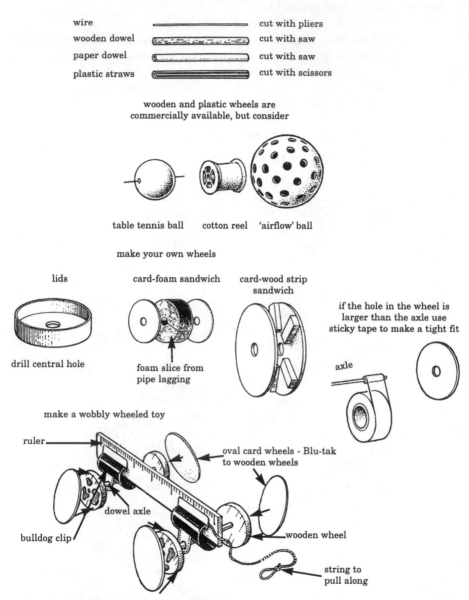

axles can be made from

wire		cut with pliers
wooden dowel		cut with saw
paper dowel		cut with saw
plastic straws		cut with scissors

wooden and plastic wheels are commercially available, but consider

table tennis ball   cotton reel   'airflow' ball

make your own wheels

lids

card-foam sandwich

card-wood strip sandwich

if the hole in the wheel is larger than the axle use sticky tape to make a tight fit

drill central hole

foam slice from pipe lagging

axle

make a wobbly wheeled toy

ruler

oval card wheels - Blu-tak to wooden wheels

dowel axle

bulldog clip

wooden wheel

string to pull along

Ways of driving vehicles with on-board sources of power are described in the next section.

Harnessing Sources of Energy for Driving Models

Many models that children make in the classroom, including wheeled vehicles, can be driven by simple sources of energy such as:

- a stretched elastic band;
- a falling weight;
- a propeller on a twisted elastic band;
- an electric motor;
- a clockwork motor;
- a blown-up balloon;
- the vehicle's own weight as it rolls down a slope;
- the energy in the person pulling or pushing the model or parts of the model.

Examples of how some of these sources of energy might be harnessed in a variety of models are shown below.

Figure 4.24   Falling weight vehicle

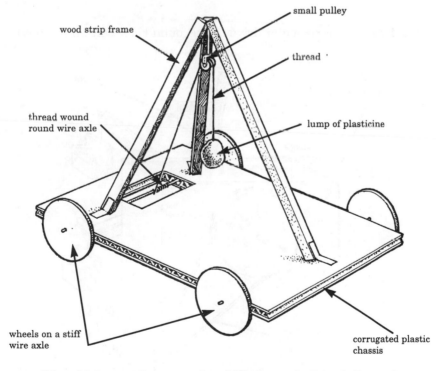

wood strip frame

small pulley

thread

thread wound round wire axle

lump of plasticine

wheels on a stiff wire axle

corrugated plastic chassis

this vehicle uses the energy in a falling mass to drive it forward

Figure 4.25   Propeller driven catamaran

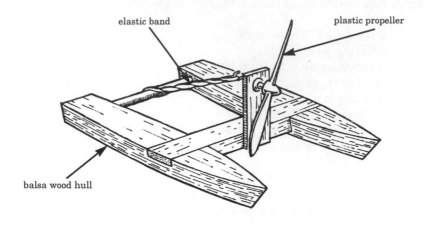

elastic band

plastic propeller

balsa wood hull

This catamaran uses the energy stored in a
twisted elastic band to move forward

Figure 4.26   Electric motor driven fairground ride (belt and pulley)

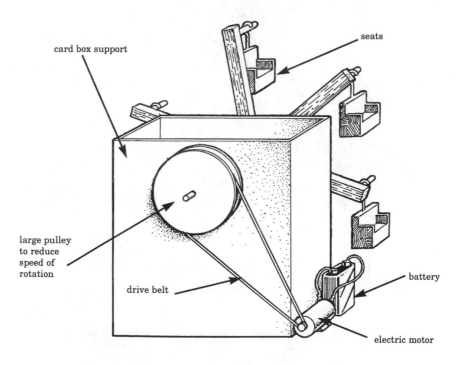

card box support

seats

large pulley
to reduce
speed of
rotation

drive belt

battery

electric motor

Figure 4.27   Balloon powered vehicle

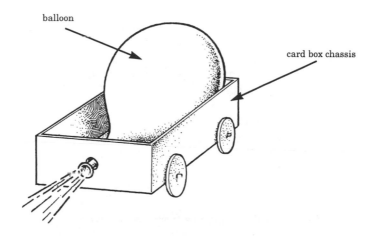

balloon

card box chassis

This vehicle uses the energy stored in the
stretched balloon to move forward

Figure 4.28   Elastic band powered game of chance

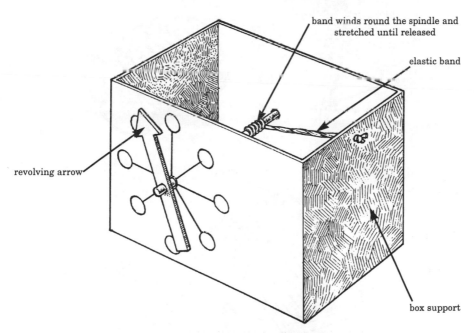

band winds round the spindle and
stretched until released

elastic band

revolving arrow

box support

This fairground game uses the energy stored in the
stretched elastic band to spin the arrow

Using Textiles in Construction

Textiles are an important material of construction in design and technology. They can be used in conjunction with other construction materials or to make products such as items of clothing on their own. They provide a strong but flexible material for components such as hinges, coverings or containers. They also possess aesthetic qualities for decorative purposes and they can be finished in a variety of unique ways such as tie dyeing, printing and embroidering. Practical capability in the use of textiles falls into a number of fields:

- Ability to cut and shape;
- Ability to join;
- Ability to finish;

Some techniques for working with textiles are illustrated below.

Figure 4.29   Making fabrics from yarn – weaving

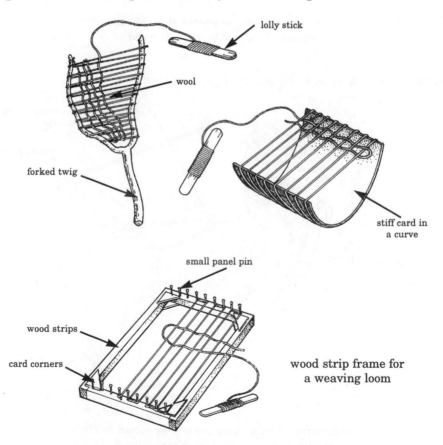

Figure 4.30   Joining fabrics – stitches etc

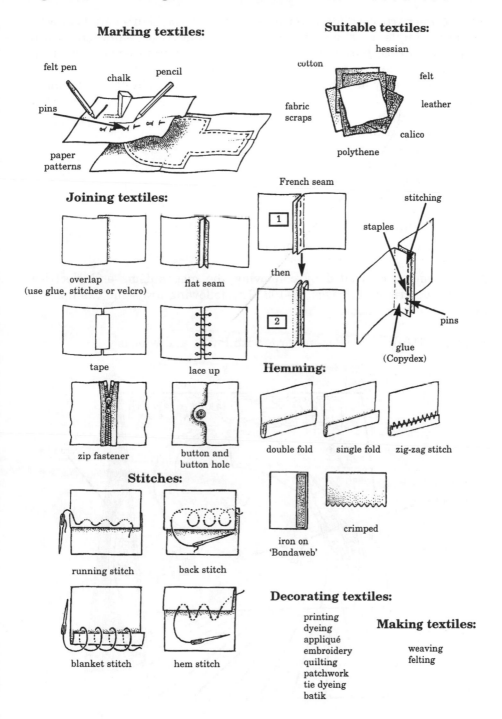

Marking textiles:

felt pen

chalk

pencil

pins

paper patterns

Suitable textiles:

hessian

cotton

felt

fabric scraps

leather

calico

polythene

Joining textiles:

overlap
(use glue, stitches or velcro)

flat seam

tape

lace up

zip fastener

button and button hole

French seam

1

then

2

stitching

staples

pins

glue
(Copydex)

Hemming:

double fold

single fold

zig-zag stitch

Stitches:

running stitch

back stitch

blanket stitch

hem stitch

iron on 'Bondaweb'

crimped

Decorating textiles:

printing
dyeing
appliqué
embroidery
quilting
patchwork
tie dyeing
batik

Making textiles:

weaving
felting

Controlling Movement

The moving parts of children's models can be controlled in a variety of ways involving simple mechanisms and sometimes electricity. Children need to gain a broad repertoire of techniques for controlling movement which can be adapted to suit a variety of circumstances.

Movement may need to be controlled when children design and make:

- a puppet;
- a toy crane;
- a model vehicle;
- a game with a moving part;
- a pop-up greetings card;
- a toy parachute;
- a model boat;
- a kite;
- a computer controlled model.

Models can be controlled by employing the mechanisms and electrical switches described on pages 89–108. The following are some examples of how this might be done.

Figure 4.31(a)   Pop-up cards with levers and wheels

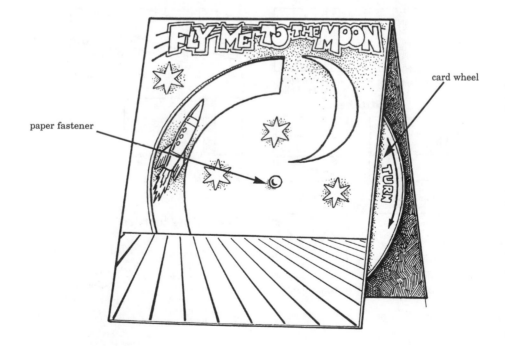

Figure 4.31(b)   Pop-up cards with levers and wheels

pull tab to move the eyes

Figure 4.32   Shadow puppet with control rods

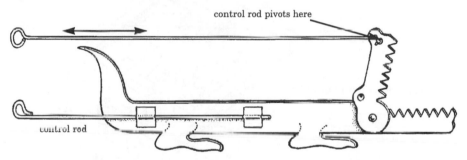

Figure 4.33   Electric powered spinning wheel with switch

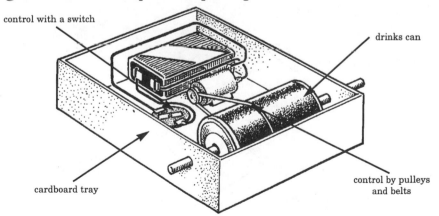

Figure 4.34   Pneumatic model with levers

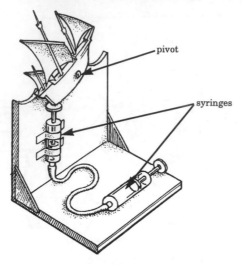

pivot

syringes

Figure 4.35   Marble maze game

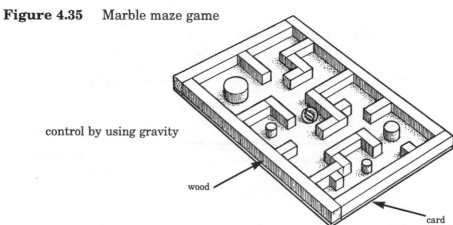

control by using gravity

wood

card

Figure 4.36   Pull along toy

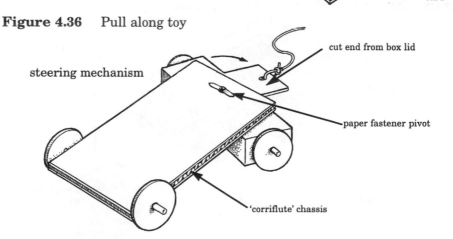

steering mechanism

cut end from box lid

paper fastener pivot

'corriflute' chassis

Part Five

Managing Design and Technology in the Primary School

Introduction

The ultimate aim of those involved with teaching design and technology in the Primary School is that children learn how to design and make products which improve the world around them and to appreciate how others have done this in the past. This learning takes place largely in the primary classroom so it is here that we must focus our efforts in developing the subject. There are a number of 'agencies' which have an effect on the child's learning in the classroom and it is these and the decisions they make that are discussed in this part. The 'agencies' having a direct effect include:

- the education authority and/or the school board of governors;
- the senior management team, including the head teacher;
- the co-ordinator for design and technology;
- the class teacher and classroom assistants.

1: Education Authority, School and Senior Management

The Education Authority and/or the School Board of Governors

The effect that this agency has on the child's learning will be largely in the form of policy decisions including those involving the school budget. The extent and nature of in-service training in curriculum subjects may also be an important area of influence. An education authority will have developed guidelines for teaching design and technology together with more specific advice for certain aspects of the subject.

Senior Management

The senior school management will be required to make decisions on a number of key issues which affect the teaching of design and technology. These involve:

- Appointing a co-ordinator for design and technology.
- Initiating part of a school development plan which identifies design and technology as a priority for development.
- Reviewing the plan at regular intervals.
- Deciding whether or not to use specialist teachers for the subject.
- Deciding how much time should be devoted to the subject.
- Deciding how the annual and weekly timetable should be structured for the whole school to suit the subject.
- Allocating resources to the subject.
- Arranging for the monitoring of progress within the subject.

THE SCHOOL DEVELOPMENT PLAN

The management team will have to decide if and when design and technology is a priority for development within the school. For instance a rolling programme might be established which maps out different subject priorities over a five year period. The rolling programme will have set periods for reviewing progress in each area. The following arguments in favour of giving design and technology a high priority might be considered:

- The subject is a new addition to the primary curriculum many teachers' minds lacks a clear definition and rationale
- The National Curriculum orders for design & technology been rewritten a number of times during their most recent development.
- The practical nature of much of the subject requires special consideration when organizing resources, including the class-room.
- It represents a process based area of the curriculum more than any other subject. Processes have been traditionally difficult to pin down and understand compared with a more content based curriculum.
- The subject develops a particular kind of skill and understanding in children which enables some of them to demonstrate a high level of ability which they may not demonstrate in other subjects. Therefore design and technology provides a balance in the curriculum which may be particularly suited to some children's learning styles and understanding.

THE USE OF SPECIALIST TEACHERS

The obvious advantage of using a specialist teacher to teach design and technology is that someone with confidence and an understanding of the subject will be able to extend the children's learning to a greater degree than a generalist classroom teacher. A specialist, teaching across a number of year groups, will gain an overview of the subject and will be in a better position to ensure continuity and progression across the subject.

There are, however, some serious disadvantages to specialist design and technology teaching in the primary school. These are:

- All design and technology would have to be timetabled into set times in the week. (If the argument for specialist teaching is extended to other subject areas, then more restrictive timetabling would be required.)
- The specialist would get to know her subject but would not be so familiar with the many children who attend the subject lessons. Learning programmes might be planned in isolation and not necessarily be related to the individual children.
- The specialist would not be in the best position to exploit the cross-curricular possibilities for the subject. A generalist class teacher will be the only one who has an overview of a particular child's learning programme. It was argued in Part 1 that design and technology could be used as a vehicle for promoting under-standing in other curriculum areas. This would be harder to achieve if specialist teaching was employed.

- All children would be taught design and technology at the same time and would generally have to proceed at a similar pace. With a class teacher, in the classroom, children can work in groups and can go on to other curriculum work if their design and technology work is completed.

Specialist teaching in the primary school has some advantages when considered in moderation. Its introduction on a wider scale, however, would have serious implications for the effective teaching of design and technology as well as other curriculum areas.

TIME DEVOTED TO DESIGN AND TECHNOLOGY

Senior management will want to define a nominal time per week which is to be devoted to design and technology which is in keeping with the total time available for all subjects and other school functions. Generally this will be between one-and-a-half hours and two hours per week throughout the year.

THE SCHOOL TIMETABLE AND THE WAY IN WHICH THIS MIGHT AFFECT DESIGN AND TECHNOLOGY

There are a number of alternative ways to timetable design and technology as with other subjects. Based on a nominal time of one-and-a-half hours per week these include:

- regular one-and-a-half hour slots each week for the whole year;
- regular two or three hour slots for a part of each year e.g. one-and-a-half terms;
- one-and-a-half hour slots over a period of consecutive days (or near consecutive days) within a one or two week period;
- whole days devoted to the subject, balanced at other times by no design and technology during the week;
- a design and technology week at given times in the year;
- combinations of the above.

There are distinct advantages to devoting more than an hour and a half slot to a design and technology activity. Because of the practical nature of the subject much time can be wasted in getting materials and tools ready and then packing them away at the end of a session. Children may suffer from a lack of continuity in their work, especially if one design and make assignment lasts over a half term or more. Teachers with less confidence in the subject might feel encouraged by the fact that more time is spent on the subject but on fewer occasions during a term.

The main disadvantage to a block of time being devoted to the subject might be that the time can be used inefficiently. The designing or making might be allowed to drag on with relatively little being gained by the children. Teachers can overcome this by structuring the block of time with regular changes of activity and discussions regarding the progress of the work. This idea is developed in the next Part when topic planning is discussed.

Much can be gained by planning a design and technology day or series of days for a number of classes together. Teachers can focus on the subject in more depth when planning the work. As a team they can support each other with ideas and organizational strategies and the accumulation of tools and materials. Classrooms can be set up for the designing and making activities and remain in this state for the duration of the project. Children can benefit from seeing what those in other classes are achieving within the same topic. The greatest benefit, however, might be the involvement of the co-ordinator for design and technology in a supportive role. The whole concentrated activity can be used as in-service training for those involved, enabling the co-ordinator to promote good practice in a real situation and within the context of the school.

SCHOOL RESOURCES FOR DESIGN AND TECHNOLOGY

Management decisions will have to be made regarding the resources available for design and technology. This will include a consideration of staffing, room space, specialist rooms, equipment including tools and materials and time made available for support and preparation.

In some schools teaching groups of children are made smaller by the addition of extra staff for design and technology. In other schools class groups remain together but an additional member of staff is made available in the classroom or specialist room. Both arrangements have timetabling implications and tend to fix the design and technology time in the week. Some schools will employ a specialist teacher for design and technology creating similar timetable restrictions.

A number of schools are finding that they can create a specialist room for design and technology or perhaps one which is shared with another subject such as science or art. A room such as this provides a useful store for materials and equipment so that, even if not all classes are able to use the room they can at least draw equipment from a central store.

2: The Co-ordinator for Design and Technology

Introduction

While it is the school management team's responsibility to establish a development plan for the whole school, the job of promoting design and technology will fall largely upon an appointed co-ordinator for the subject. The co-ordinator will be someone who has some confidence in teaching the subject and who can take a role in leading and supporting others in the school.

The role of the co-ordinator for design and technology will be one which is defined by the school management to suit the circumstances in a particular school. The character and abilities of the post holder may be taken into account when this role is defined. A co-ordinator for design and technology in a primary school might be expected to carry out some or all of the following duties:

- to provide personal examples of good practice within the subject by using sound teaching methods and displaying children's work;
- to provide general encouragement for colleagues in teaching the subject;
- to co-ordinate the running of the subject within the school by collaborating with year groups or phase groups;
- to develop a school policy for design and technology in consultation with other members of staff;
- to develop a scheme of work for design and technology;
- to provide support for colleagues in teaching design and technology;
- to monitor the progress of the subject within the school;
- to order and maintain materials and equipment and to plan for suitable storage and distribution of these;
- to provide advice on the allocation of other resources such as space, furniture, staffing, and time;
- to consult with the head teacher, advisory teachers, independent consultants and the Education Authority regarding the subject;
- to be conversant with the relevant literature on the subject including:

Education Authority reports and papers;
government reports;
subject association literature;
commercial publications such as books, journals and magazines;
press reports;

- to attend relevant subject courses, conferences and exhibitions and encourage others to do so;
- to liaise with pre-school providers, feeder schools, parallel primary schools and high schools;
- to join and/or be aware of subject associations for design and technology. For example, The Design and Technology Association (DATA), The Design Council.

Two of the key jobs carried out by the co-ordinator involve supporting colleagues in teaching the subject and monitoring progress. These are described in detail later in this Part. The development of a policy, scheme of work and topic planning are dealt with in Part 6.

Developing Design and Technology as Part of the School Development Plan

If the development of design and technology is identified as having a high priority in the overall school development plan then a number of steps might be taken by the co-ordinator in order to establish the action necessary:

- Carry out a curriculum audit involving the current scheme for design and technology as well as the current resources.
- Identify areas for development within design and technology.
- Prioritize these areas of concern.
- Draw up an action plan with delegated responsibilities and including a date for reviewing progress.
- Evaluate the action taken and make further plans if necessary.

Curriculum Audit

Newly appointed co-ordinators of design and technology, whether they be familiar with the running of the school or not, will need to explore, in a formal way, the way in which the subject is already being taught. It is a wise strategy to build upon what already exists rather than try to make a sudden and radical change all at once. A survey of existing practice might include the following:

- existing school policy documents;
- existing school schemes of work;
- assessment of pupils' abilities;
- recording of pupils' work;
- equipment – both hardware and software;
- how has equipment been used in past?
- how is it used now?
- published schemes of work and/or text books available in school;
- examples of good practice in the classroom;
- staff expertise;
- staff interests.

A questionnaire can be used to find out some of this information but this should be well designed and not too demanding of teachers' time. Person to person contact and conversation is a much better way to gather information because it eliminates much misunderstanding and often provides extra, useful information. The conversations with staff can be given greater structure if the co-ordinator has a list of concerns sketched out beforehand.

A survey of this nature can raise the profile of the subject and provide a sound basis for making decisions about it in the future. A formal audit is often especially necessary if the teacher is new to the school or new to the post of co-ordinator. However, teachers who have served for some time in a school will often be surprised what they can learn about their school and the way it functions once they focus on one subject area in detail.

Identifying Areas for Development

The senior management team may have identified design and technology as a subject with a high priority for development. If this is so it will fall upon the co-ordinator to consider the areas within design and technology that might require development. These areas might include those outlined on the opposite page. The individual sections shown can be used as a basis for establishing a priority for each area. Blank spaces have been included so that schools can enter areas of concern specific to their own establishment.

Figure 5.1 Table to show possible areas of concern within design and technology

Classroom organization	Creating a school policy
Creating more lesson ideas	Cross-curricular links with design and technology
Differentiation and special needs	Encouraging classroom display
Equal opportunities	Establishing progression and continuity
Exploring links between science and design and technology	Formative teacher assessment and recording
Improving teachers' confidence	Increasing teachers' background knowledge and understanding
Increasing teachers' practical capability	Increasing teachers' understanding of the processes of designing and making
National curriculum interpretation and requirements	Obtaining more equipment and material resources
Organizing the storage and distribution of existing resources	Planning structured learning experiences
Summative teacher assessment and reporting to parents	Timetable requirements for design and technology
Use of IT to support design & technology	Writing a scheme of work for the whole school
Carry out a curriculum audit	

Prioritizing

The co-ordinator, together with the school management team, will want to establish some form of priority over the aspects of design and technology that need to be tackled in any one development period. There are many jobs to be done in developing this new curriculum area and it would be a mistake to try to tackle everything at once. One technique for establishing priorities is the Diamond 9 activity described below This could be carried out between the head and the co-ordinator or include a wider selection of staff in a staff meeting.

Diamond 9 Activity

This simple activity can be used with a group who are trying to establish an order of priority for developing various aspects of school work.

1　Take nine pieces of paper or card, about postcard size.

2　Write out as fully as possible, on each card, the distinct areas of concern which have to be prioritized.

3　Choose the one card which represents the task with highest priority and place this at the apex of the diamond.

4　Choose two more tasks which are near enough equally second in priority and place these under the first card.

5　Continue like this until you have formed a diamond where each level represents a decreasing level of importance. (Clearly alternative shapes can be formed such as a triangle if necessary.)

THE ACTION PLAN

Having established one or two high priority areas for development within the subject, an informal plan could be discussed for tackling the problems involved. Some co-ordinators and head teachers, however, might find it of benefit to have a record of what is to be done together with who is responsible for doing this. If a timescale is established then a date for reviewing progress can be set. An example of an action plan for developing the curriculum is shown on page 168.

Figure 5.2   An example of a Diamond 9 activity

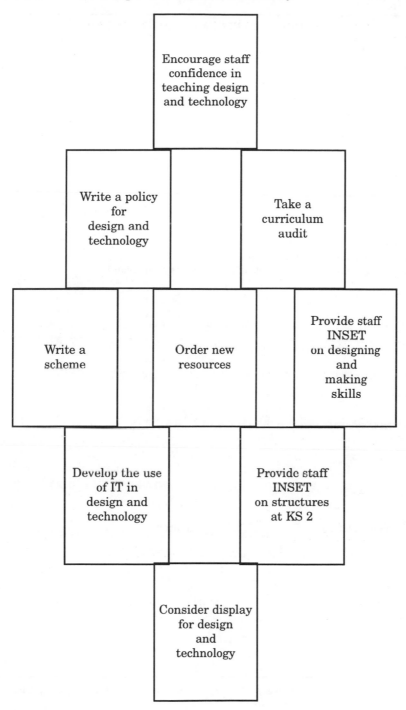

Figure 5.3   School development action plan

SCHOOL DEVELOPMENT ACTION PLAN

Subject:

Date:

Person responsible for overseeing plan:

Completed by:

Monitored by:

Objectives and success criteria for the plan:
(These will be employed in evaluating the outcomes of the plan.)

-

-

-

-

-

Short description of the action to be taken.

People to be involved   Capacity

Resources required:

Adapted from *School Development Planning in the Primary School* Coventry City Council Support and Advisory Service, 1995

Reviewing Progress

So much happens in one term within a school that many worthy plans and actions can get swallowed up and overwhelmed. Setting a time to review the progress of plans helps to keep these on track and to ensure that eventually the aims are met. Building in a time for reflection half way through a long term plan is a good idea and enables slight readjustments of the time scale to be made in the light of new developments.

If clear objectives were stated in the action plan then an evaluation of the success or otherwise of the development programme can easily be made. One advantage of an action plan together with an evaluation is that even if things didn't go as planned there is clear evidence that something was being done about a particular issue. Staff might find it encouraging to look back over a period such as a school year and realize just how much has been achieved in a short space of time. A brief, written record of this is provided by the plan and evaluation.

An example of a simple evaluating form is shown on the next page.

SCHOOL DEVELOPMENT PLAN

EVALUATION AND UPDATE

Subject:

Date:

Development plan issue From (date):	Achieved (Which objectives have been met?)	Outstanding

Adapted from *School Development Planning in the Primary School* Coventry City Council Support and Advisory Service, 1995

Figure 5.4   School development plan evaluation

Supporting Colleagues in Teaching Design and Technology

One of the most important and effective jobs that a co-ordinator does is to support colleagues in teaching the subject. The support can take many forms ranging from a quick, encouraging chat in the staff room about a successful lesson carried out that day to a formal presentation and workshop on a staff training day. The emphasis should be on the positive reinforcement of good practice and encouragement to progress towards a better understanding of the subject. It is important that the co-ordinator sets a good example of what is possible within the school's own context and points out examples of what others have achieved (perhaps with a different year group).

The following strategies might be employed by the co-ordinator in supporting colleagues in design and technology.

BE ENCOURAGING ABOUT THE DESIGN AND TECHNOLOGY COLLEAGUES ARE CURRENTLY DOING

Human beings thrive on *genuine* encouragement but often react negatively towards criticism. With this thought in mind it is worth considering the circumstance in which encouragement can be given. The co-ordinator must become aware of the design and technology which is going on elsewhere in the school. This can be done through informal conversations in the staff room, noticing classroom displays, talking to year group co-ordinators about their termly plans and identifying appropriate elements of design and technology in such occasions as school assemblies.

Examples of good practice carried out by others provide powerful arguments for what is possible in the subject within the actual school setting. These also show what can be done by a 'non-specialist' teacher. If examples of children's work can be collected and stored these may be useful later when promoting the subject in, say, a staff meeting.

THE USE OF DISPLAY

One way of promoting a curriculum area is to arrange effective displays of children's work. The co-ordinator will initially arrange these in her classroom but more impact will be gained by displaying in corridors or entrance halls. The work children do in design and technology lends itself to three dimensional as well as two dimensional display. This is an added attraction. A co-ordinator can illustrate a number of key features of a subject by using some carefully planned display work. For instance a process skill such as *evaluating* can be shown to involve a variety of sub-skills by displaying children's written work alongside the products which were evaluated.

Eventually the co-ordinator will want to encourage others to display work in design and technology but this can only be reasonably achieved if she has 'led the way'. Static displays are not the only way in which work can be shown off. The use of puppets or other props in an assembly would provide an excellent focus for children's work in design and technology. Much can be gained by witnessing the pleasure expressed by children as they describe how and why something was designed and made.

MEETINGS WITH INDIVIDUALS AND GROUPS

Curriculum development meetings with individuals or groups provide an excellent forum for discussing a particular curriculum area. The obvious group to address is the year group or phase group who are just about to plan a topic involving design and technology. The co-ordinator's involvement in other teachers' planning means a lot of hard work but the benefits are enormous both from a supportive point of view and a monitoring one.

Less formal discussions with individuals are often less threatening and just as rewarding. Co-ordinators need to make it clear that they are available for such discussions and that they positively welcome them.

WORKING ALONGSIDE OTHERS IN THE CLASSROOM

One of the most powerful ways in which a subject co-ordinator can achieve her objectives is to work alongside teachers in their own classroom. This demands that time be given to a co-ordinator for this but there are many benefits to such an arrangement. The time allocated only needs to be one hour or a little longer per week and there is no reason why the co-ordinator should not work with different colleagues over a period of, say, a term. If the co-ordinator takes the lead in the lesson, but is supported by the class teacher then neither should feel too threatened by the situation.

One advantage of such an arrangement is that the co-ordinator, through planning with the class teacher, will be able to discuss many issues concerning the subject. Subject content, classroom management and safe procedures can all be considered. The co-ordinator will benefit from experience with a different age group, thus adding credibility to her plans for the whole primary age range which are set out in the scheme. If the class teacher is willing to pass on the ideas to the rest of a year group team then this becomes an effective way to disseminate ideas and philosophies.

The main advantages of such an arrangement is that the co-ordinator becomes free to explore design ideas with a group of children in the presence of their class teacher, while the teacher is temporarily relieved of full responsibility for the content of the subject. It can add up to an enjoyable experience if time can be found to do it.

USE A QUESTIONNAIRE TO HIGHLIGHT ISSUES

There are a number of ways in which co-ordinators can highlight issues concerning their subject within the school. One way is to create a questionnaire which might help in making a curriculum audit. By asking sensitively phrased questions, the co-ordinator will be able to find out information about the state of design and technology in the school. At the same time, however, she will be prompting colleagues to think a little more closely about their own classroom practice. A question such as 'How do you store the resources for design and technology in your classroom?' will prompt the teacher to consider which resources should be devoted to the subject as well as provide information about storage facilities.

DESIGN AND TECHNOLOGY EVENTS

An appreciation of design and technology can be enhanced by planning special events such as a shared design and technology day or week. Sometimes a year group or phase or even the whole school can take part in a day of activities centred around one subject. This idea enables teachers as well as children to get to grips with what is involved. From the co-ordinator's point of view it provides an ideal opportunity to support colleagues in a constructive and practical way.

In some schools it may be appropriate to stage a parents' evening at which design and technology is a major feature. If a practical problem solving approach is taken then a light hearted competitive element can enliven the proceedings. Such an event will give the school a chance to explain a new curriculum area to parents, demonstrate possible links with industry and involve parents in an understanding of how their children learn in school.

ORGANIZE RESOURCES EFFECTIVELY

A key job for the co-ordinator of design and technology will be to order, maintain and make available suitable resources. The resources include tools, materials and suitable publications as well as room space if this is available. The co-ordinator will need to monitor the use of equipment and be prepared to have repairs made if this becomes necessary.

Resources may be held in a central area such as the co-ordinator's classroom, a specialist area or a cupboard in the corridor. A system for distribution will be required which all staff understand and can use. Alternatively resources might be distributed among individual classrooms or groups of classrooms. This should require less monitoring and rely more on the groups to maintain and distribute.

Suitable publications might include national curriculum documents, teachers' books, pupils' books, technology schemes, journals and magazines and publications made available by the local Education Authority. These would be best kept centrally in a staff room library with a system for checking publications in and out.

IN-SERVICE TRAINING BY THE CO-ORDINATOR

More formal in-service training can be given by the co-ordinator, either during a staff meeting or on a staff training day. This can take many forms, from a discussion about the principles behind the subject to a series of practical workshops. Generally it is a good idea to mix practical work with a chance to discuss and reflect. The following points are worth considering before embarking on the provision of in-service training for staff:

In the beginning:

- Identify and be clear about the needs of the participants.
- Consider providing ideas or papers before the meeting so that staff can think these over.
- Ensure that you *build* on the experiences, interests and needs of the staff.
- Try to encourage the audience to take ownership of new ideas rather than dictate these.
- Consider the usefulness of individuals learning from each other through group discussion.
- Think about how you will arrange the learning environment to suit the type of learning going on.
- Think about how you can use a variety of teaching methods.
- Don't plan to talk for too long.
- Provide *doing* activities as well as looking and listening.
- Consider using other people (both visitors and participants) as a learning resource.

Getting started:

- It is a good idea to begin with an overview of the session or series of sessions.
- Be flexible in timetabling the parts of the learning session, responding to needs as they arise.
- Be willing to listen to and respond to others' viewpoints even when they are unexpected.
- Use praise and encouragement and generally build confidence.

Finally:

- At the end, provide a clear summary of the main ideas.
- Make some form of evaluation of the session, possibly by asking the staff to note down their views.

EXAMPLE OF AN INSET ACTIVITY

There are many forms of in-service activities which the co-ordinator can provide for a staff. The following is an example of one such activity which illustrates how a mixture of teaching styles can be used to approach a difficult concept. It is based on the need to understand the process of designing and making.

INSET ACTIVITY – DESIGNING AND MAKING SKILLS

The following is a simple INSET activity which can be used with staff in a school to enable them to consider the nature of design and technology and the procedural skills involved. The idea is that a number of different, short design and make tasks are tackled by groups of staff. This should be good fun but at the same time very informative. In each case an observer notes down the skills being used on a prepared sheet. These skills are shared within the group at the end.

Prepare some simple equipment for each design task being used.

1   Explain that the following activity will help to answer the question: When people are designing and making, what skills are used?
2   Divide the staff into groups of three – two designers and one observer.
3   Ask the observers from each group to read through the Observer's Guide sheet. (They need a little time to digest the information on this sheet.) Observers might write on the sheet under each heading or use the blank reverse side of the sheet to record their observations.
4   When the observers are ready, give them the Design Task for their group on a slip of paper. Let them read this and ask them to get their group started.
5   Circulate, providing words of encouragement, but try not to get involved in the activity itself.
6   After about 15 minutes it is worth giving a 5 minute warning with a comment that it is not essential that all the tasks are completed.
7   After about 20 minutes ask designers to stop and observers to show the sheet they have been using and the observations they have made. This should be a two way discussion and a general sharing of ideas.
8   Gather all groups together and identify the broad skills used in designing and making.

DESIGN TASKS

Identification

When you are at a party, a meeting or a conference it often helps to know everyone's name and something of their character.

Devise a fun way of identifying others who are meeting for the first time. Use the simple materials available to make the device to fit yourself and others in your group.

Hat

Make a 'fun' hat with the materials available. Decide who it is designed for and the occasion on which that person would wear it.

Pencil Holder

Pencils and pens will often roll off a sloping table. Use the materials available to make something which stops this happening.

Make your invention easy to use on a variety of work surfaces.

OBSERVER'S GUIDE

Note down examples of:

- the participants clarifying their task – *'What exactly is meant by this?'*;
- the participants deciding on certain features for their model in advance *i.e. its size, its appearance, its functioning parts, who it is for, its general purpose;*
- the participants thinking of a number of ideas before settling on just one to pursue;
- different ways of communicating ideas – *talking, drawing, waving hands around, etc.;*
- using the provided materials to try ideas out;
- gathering information related to the task – *asking questions, reading, listening to advice etc.;*
- evaluation of the project as it proceeds;
- deciding in which order to do things;
- allowance for the constraints of time;
- construction skills used – *measuring and marking out, cutting, shaping, joining, finishing;*
- some ways of testing the model;
- improvements to the model;
- some form of evaluation of the finished product and the way in which it was made.

Note down any other types of activity not listed here.

INVITING VISITING SPEAKERS

In addition to the co-ordinator providing in-service training for the staff in a school, it may be a good idea to invite others into the school to carry out a similar function. Sometimes an outside agency, such as an advisory teacher or independent consultant, can be used to reinforce the message that the co-ordinator is constantly giving.

ATTENDING COURSES, CONFERENCES AND EXHIBITIONS

The co-ordinator might also consider encouraging other staff members to attend in-service courses outside of the school. These may take a variety of forms from Education Authority courses to one day conferences organized by regional groups for design and technology. A number of national and regional exhibitions include ideas and publications for design and technology and some groups organize problem-solving competitions all of which will add to an overall appreciation of the subject.

Monitoring the Development of Design and Technology

An increasingly important function of the subject co-ordinator is the monitoring of the development of a subject in a school. Monitoring has always occurred in an informal way but techniques for doing this need to be strengthened in the future. Monitoring is about gathering information about how well the subject is being organized and taught and learnt by children. DATA (1995a) identify three strands to monitoring:

- monitoring intentions;
- monitoring practice;
- monitoring effectiveness.

The intentions for design and technology are set out in the school policy, scheme of work, topic plans and individual lesson plans. The practice is a measure of what actually happens and how well this was achieved. The effectiveness relates to the quality of children's learning as measured in teacher assessment and standard tests. The quality of teaching would be monitored as part of the effectiveness of the subject provision. The co-ordinator may also want to monitor the effect of the support for the subject provided by the co-ordinator and others in the school.

There a number of strategies which will enable co-ordinators to monitor their subject.

MEETING COLLEAGUES FORMALLY

Staff meetings, phase meetings or year group meetings may be used to discuss and review the scheme, forward topic plans or individual lesson plans.

TEACHING ALONGSIDE COLLEAGUES

This is described in the section on supporting colleagues. It requires time but provides an effective method of monitoring colleagues' understanding of the subject.

ASSISTING COLLEAGUES AS THEY TEACH

The co-ordinator becomes an assistant while the member of staff takes the lead in the lesson.

OBSERVING COLLEAGUES AS THEY TEACH

This method and the one above put the onus on the non-specialist teacher to teach in front of another member of staff. This may be considered too threatening to be acceptable to many and requires time to be made available to the co-ordinator. The co-ordinator plays less of a supporting role, thus losing one of the advantages which might be gained from being in the same classroom as a colleague.

CREATING AN AWARD SYSTEM FOR GOOD WORK BY CHILDREN

A system whereby teachers in a school send children who have done well in design and technology to the co-ordinator for praise can have its benefits. It can encourage all children and enables the co-ordinator to become familiar with good practice and learning within the school.

HAVING INFORMAL CONVERSATIONS WITH COLLEAGUES

Teachers often respond well to those who express a genuine interest in their work especially if they receive positive feedback from this.

INITIATING STAFF DISCUSSIONS IN MEETINGS

Much can be revealed if discussions about a subject are handled sensitively, with no-one feeling threatened, but everyone feeling their contributions are valued.

LOOKING AT CHILDREN'S WORK

A regular survey of the products children make in other classrooms and the records they make during its progress can give an insight into how children are learning within the subject.

LOOKING AT CLASSROOM DISPLAYS

Other teachers' displays will often reveal a great deal about how the subject was approached and can provide a starting point for further discussions.

MONITORING ASSESSMENT RECORDS FOR ALL CHILDREN

The co-ordinator may have the job of collecting records of formal assessment for all the children in a school. This will provide an overview of abilities within the school which can be compared with a national average.

MONITORING TOPIC AND LESSON PLANS FOR DESIGN AND TECHNOLOGY

In some schools it is the co-ordinator's responsibility to pre-view all forward plans for their subject. This allows them to discuss possibilities with staff that, perhaps, they were not aware of.

ORGANIZING A DESIGN AND TECHNOLOGY DAY/WEEK IN WHICH GROUPS COLLABORATE AND SHARE IDEAS

The sharing of a common experience, such as a technology day, enables the co-ordinator to get a feel for how others are approaching the subject.

ORGANIZING DISPLAYS OF WORK AT PARENTS' EVENINGS OR DURING ASSEMBLIES

As with classroom displays, displays of work at parents' evenings or in the assembly hall will often reveal a great deal about an individual teacher's approach to a subject and can provide a focus for further discussion.

RECORDING THE FREQUENCY OF USE OF EQUIPMENT AND OTHER RESOURCES

Systems for distributing equipment may have a monitoring device built in to them. This will enable the co-ordinator to order appropriate resources in the future.

TALKING TO CHILDREN ABOUT THEIR WORK IN DESIGN AND TECHNOLOGY

If this is done sensitively, it can reveal information about children's learning as well as their attitude to the subject.

USING A QUESTIONNAIRE

Questionnaires can be used to collect opinions or factual data about a subject. It gives each individual member of staff a confidential voice and at the same time can prompt them to consider things they had so far taken for granted.

Preparing for School Inspections

Schools and individual subjects may be inspected by various agencies such as the Office for Standards in Education (OFSTED) or advisory teachers from the Local Education Authority. Much of the information that the inspectors gain will be through reading the school's written documentation, but in addition to this it is likely that the co-ordinator for a subject will be interviewed. The following issues might be discussed in such an interview and the co-ordinator for design and technology might want to prepare for such an event.

QUESTIONS WHICH MAY BE PUT TO A CO-ORDINATOR DURING AN INSPECTION

Curriculum documentation

- Are the essential elements of the school policy in place?
- Are schemes of work and topic plans in place?
- When were these documents produced?
- When will aspects of them be reviewed?
- How were the curriculum documents produced?
- Are you satisfied with the documentation?

The co-ordinator's role

- How long have you acted as co-ordinator for the subject?
- What, in your view, is your job description?
- Is this information formally recorded?
- How does this job description match with what you actually do?
- Can you give examples of how you support colleagues within the subject?
- Are you involved in monitoring and evaluating the subject. Give examples;
- Is time allocated to you to carry out your co-ordinator's responsibilities. About how much?

School development planning

- Describe how the subject has featured in any recent school development plan;
- What are the strengths of the subject within your school?
- What are the weaknesses?
- What are the development priorities for the subject?
- Are any areas in development at the moment?
- When will this development be reviewed?

Quality of teaching

- Do you have an overview of the quality of teaching within the whole school?
- Comment on teachers' ability to plan a broad programme of work which is suited to differing abilities;
- How would you rate the confidence of the teachers in this subject?
- What are the needs of the teachers in developing this subject?

Quality of learning

- Do you have an overview of the quality of learning within the subject throughout the school?
- What are the general attitudes of the pupils to the subject?
- Do you have an overview of the pupils' standards of achievement in the subject?
- How do you gather evidence of these standards?

Assessment recording and reporting

- What are the assessment, recording and reporting arrangements for the subject?
- How is pupil assessment moderated?

Staff development

- How are the in-service needs of the staff identified and prioritized within the subject?
- How do you, or others, provide in-service training for colleagues?
- What in-service training in the subject have you personally received in the past five years?
- What are your future needs in this area?

Resources

- Do you have complete responsibility for resources?
- Do you feel you have sufficient resources?
- How are funds made available for resources? How much is this?
- How do you identify resource requirements for the whole staff?
- How do you order, store, distribute and maintain resources?
- What use is made of resources outside school?
- Is the accommodation in school generally sufficient?
- How does the accommodation affect the teaching and learning within the subject?
- Does the way in which the subject is timetabled reflect the requirements of the subject?

(Adapted from Coventry Education Authority literature.)

An inspection of any kind may seem a daunting prospect, largely because so much information has to be gathered and communicated to the inspector. This information often exists in schools but not in a readily communicable form. If the inspection is viewed as a way of identifying and clarifying the way in which a school should develop in the future then it can be seen as a positive exercise which will benefit all.

3:   The Class Teacher

Introduction

The class teacher has a key role in managing learning in design and technology within the classroom. This will involve a consideration of the following:

- planning and assessing learning activities;
- the classroom layout;
- the use of specialist rooms;
- grouping children;
- the classroom timetable;
- availability of resources for children;
- storage of resources and partly finished products.

Topic and lesson planning for design and technology is dealt with in Part Six – Curriculum Planning and Documentation. These plans will be influenced by a number of other decisions that the teacher makes and the constraints within which she is working. Teachers need to create space in their classrooms for practical activities to take place and may need to provide protective covering for desks for some tasks.

The Classroom Layout

Many resources that children use when designing and making will already be to hand in a normal primary classroom. Tools such as pencils, rulers, scissors and hole punches will be available. Materials such as paper, card, adhesive tape and recycled materials will be used throughout the curriculum. Class teachers should consider the benefits of making these basic tools and materials available for all children at all times so that these can be chosen when required. It is important that teachers' time is not taken up unnecessarily in finding and replacing basic resources. Children can be trained from an early age to collect, use and maintain many basic items in the classroom. One might argue that this open availability (with suitable constraints applied) should be a feature of the open-ended nature of many design and technology tasks.

Children should be taught to respect the value of materials and not waste these, and to handle tools and space in a safe and efficient way. The availability of materials has an important effect on the way in which children design their products. It was argued in Part Two that a knowledge of what is available will significantly influence the design proposals that children produce. It is when the materials of construction are not on display that children's design proposals become unrealistic, limited and often do not resemble the final product which *was* made with greater knowledge of the materials available.

Specialist Rooms

Some schools will have a specialist room set aside for design and technology which will almost certainly be timetabled for use. The class teacher together with the co-ordinator will have to decide if the benefits of using the room are greater than the advantages of using the classroom. A specialist room can be set out with suitable resources, including water, an uncarpeted floor and heavy duty work surfaces. Displays can be targeted at the skills and knowledge required by the children in that subject. The children may be motivated and stimulated by the use of a room other than their usual classroom.

Grouping Children

The disadvantages of using a specialist room are that it will probably have to be used at a fixed time in the week for a set duration. Part-finished models may have to be transported to and from the classroom. The room will almost certainly have to be maintained by the co-ordinator since no one else will 'own' the room. It will probably require the teacher to teach design and technology to the whole group at the same time. This factor, however, will be seen by some as an advantage. In the classroom small groups of children can do design and technology while others are given work in other curricular areas. This may enable the teacher to give greater attention to a smaller group while they carry out practical work. Children who complete their work in design and technology in the classroom can easily be directed towards another task such as finishing work from a previous day.

The Classroom Timetable

The classroom timetable may be flexible enough for the class teacher to arrange design and technology during a period when there are no inconvenient breaks in the middle of work. Some teachers, however, may find that a break in the middle of practical work is an advantage. Some class teachers, especially at Key Stage 1, may find they can arrange their timetable so that children are given time to complete an extended piece of work over a few days and then to balance this with less design and technology in a subsequent week. This flexibility will certainly be an advantage to the subject.

Further constraints to the classroom timetable will be met if additional teachers or classroom assistants are employed to help with a more practical subject or if the co-ordinator for design and technology is to work alongside the class teacher during a specified time. The advantages of additional teachers and adult assistants, however, far outweigh the disadvantages of tighter timetabling and does not prevent a more flexible approach when this facility is not available.

Part Six

Curriculum Planning and Documentation

Introduction

Design and technology in the primary school is a new and emerging area of study. Its evolution within a school will occur in uneven, sometimes unpredictable, stages. It is important to recognize that curriculum development is not a neat and tidy process which begins with a clearly laid out policy and proceeds through the development of a scheme of work and topic plans to ideal lesson plans. Note also that a clearly set out school policy on any curriculum area cannot be written until thinking has become clear on the subject. This clear thinking can only be developed through practice and experience, so the final policy may emerge at the same time as or even after the outlines of a scheme have been developed. Most schools will find that some time is spent in trialling a variety of small topics and lessons in design and technology before a coherent and progressive scheme is developed. This is to be expected and should not be undervalued.

This Part will explore the development of a school policy, scheme of work, topic planning and finally lesson planning within a school. Advice will be given on assessment, differentiation and progression in design and technology.

The four elements which lead to a fully planned curriculum in design and technology might be represented in the following way.

Figure 6.1   Curriculum planning documents

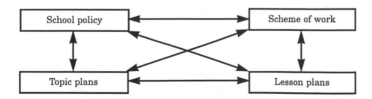

187

1: Writing a Policy and Scheme of Work for Design and Technology

The Policy Document

A school policy for design and technology should provide a 'guiding light' for all those involved in teaching the subject within a school. At the same time it provides a record of the approach to the subject that the school, as a whole, has adopted. Visitors to the school such as parents, governors; other teachers or OFSTED inspectors might use this document to get a feel for the direction in which the subject is being developed. It should be particularly helpful to teachers who are new to a school by giving them an idea of how they are expected to teach. It is a good idea to write any policy with these particular audiences in mind. The policy should not be so detailed that it begins to encroach upon the information laid out in the scheme of work. The essential elements in a policy for design and technology are as follows:

Definition for design and technology

This might involve a quote from another publication or a personal view. Use some of the wording from the National Curriculum orders.

A rationale for teaching the subject

Why should design and technology be taught in this particular school? What are the benefits for doing so?

The broad aims which will be achieved by teaching design and technology

Include a limited number of broad aims for design and technology which are in keeping with the broad aims of the school and the requirements of the National Curriculum, if appropriate.

The more specific objectives which should be met by the children in the school

These should be based on the programmes of study in the National Curriculum, if appropriate, and could be written in the form:

By the time the children have completed their time in this school they should have . . .

Time allocation for design and technology

How much time per week should be devoted to the subject? How will this time be distributed throughout the year?

Management of design and technology

Who has responsibility for various aspects of the subject such as ordering equipment and planning in-service training?

Classroom organization

This includes recommendations as to how the subject should be organized in the classroom. Comment on pupil groups, the use of specialist rooms and storage of equipment etc.

Resources

Which resources are available and how will these be ordered, organized and maintained?

Assessment, recording and reporting policy

How will pupils' achievements in the subject be assessed? Which assessment techniques ought to be employed? Is there a policy for marking children's work? How will achievements be recorded and reported to the children themselves, other teachers and parents?

Teaching styles and approaches

Which special teaching styles should be employed in design and technology? Comment on the open-ended approach to design and make tasks and the practical nature of much of the subject.

Progression and continuity

Outline the way in which progression and continuity will be ensured through use of a carefully developed scheme.

Differentiation

Discuss ways in which children of all abilities can be catered for within the subject.

Cross curricular links

Identify the need to establish and exploit cross-curricular links. Highlight occasions when this might be possible.

Equal opportunities

State a policy which includes all groups within the school community.

Health and safety

List the safety rules which are appropriate to the school and to the facilities available.

Staff development

Describe the policy for staff development in design and technology, including how staff needs might be identified.

Monitoring and reviewing

Describe arrangements whereby the scheme can be regularly monitored and provide a mechanism for making periodic reviews.

Various aspects of the policy for design and technology should conform to whole school policies in a range of areas such as assessment, cross-curricular links and equal opportunities.

Developing a Scheme for Design and Technology

It will often fall upon the co-ordinator to develop a scheme for design and technology. A scheme of work for the whole school will provide a detailed account, term by term, of what can be expected to happen in each classroom regarding the subject. It is not necessarily a collection of topic or lesson plans but should provide enough information for individual teachers to make these plans themselves. A carefully thought-out scheme will enable a visitor to the school to obtain an overview of everything that goes on in that subject throughout the year.

A major function of a scheme is to ensure that learning programmes become progressively more demanding as a child develops throughout the school. This progression and the continuity associated with this will ensure that children are given the opportunity to become better and better at the subject and will avoid them having to unnecessarily repeat experiences.

A well written scheme will ensure breadth of experiences within the subject and will indicate how these experiences link with other subjects and cross-curricular themes.

In almost all schools there will be some design and technology going on before a coherent scheme is developed. There may be the outline of a scheme which has become out of date or there may be conflicting schemes developed by different groups within the school. Alternatively an already successful scheme may need revising. A new scheme, then, will almost always be developed from practice which already exists. It makes a great deal of sense to take this into account when writing the new scheme rather that trying to ignore this and start afresh. The chances are that there will be some teachers who are very pleased with the design and technology they already do with their children and would not want to abandon this because of some arbitrary decisions made when a new scheme was produced in isolation.

A new scheme, then, will take account of the needs of the whole school but will develop from a variety of constraints which might already exist. These might be:

- the maintenance of successful practice which already exists within the school;
- the cross-curricular topics adopted by each year group;
- a scheme for part of the school which must remain intact;
- the desire to use a published scheme;
- the demands of feeder schools and High schools.

Once these constraints have been accounted for there are a number of ways of developing the scheme which are outlined below.

GETTING STARTED

When starting to develop a scheme for the whole school, a blank sheet of paper can be very intimidating. The following are some suggestions for overcoming this 'writer's block'.

Set out a grid – like the one on the next page – using a large sheet of paper.

1   If your school has a rolling programme of two or three years for its timetable then adapt the table accordingly. Also if your school prefers to change topic every term then omit the central lines for each term.
2   Note down on the outline scheme any constraints such as fixed cross-curricular themes throughout the year or, for example, the need to always do Electricity in year 5 in the Autumn term.
3   Decide on which of the following to base the scheme for design and technology:

- Topic themes:
    cross-curricular themes e.g. the weather;
    design and technology themes e.g. toys;
- Design and make assignments;
- Practical capability (manipulative) skills (such as how to use scissors or construct a wood strip frame);
- Emphasis on key design and make process skills (such as modelling, evaluating or researching):
- The materials used;
- Published schemes.

With a view to the appropriateness of any one of these starting points for a particular year group as well as achieving progression and breadth of experience, enter these on the grid. The example opposite shows you how.

Figure 6.2   Grid for outline scheme

Outline scheme for design and technology						
YEAR	TERM 1		TERM 2		TERM 3	
R						
1						
2						
3						
4						
5						
6						

Figure 6.3   Example 1: Taking design and technology themes as a starting point:

Outline scheme for design and technology						
YEAR	**TERM 1**		**TERM 2**		**TERM 3**	
R			Monsters and Dragons	My lunch	Finger puppets	
1	Postman Pat	Christmas decorations	Furniture for a doll's house		Picnic	
2	Toys		Greetings cards		Sunny holidays	
3	The weather		Shops and shopping	Containers	Bridges and towers	
4	Using electricity		Games	Puppets	The fairground	
5	Protective clothing		Outdoor adventure		The garden	
6	Celebrations		Computer control		The local environment	

In the example above, some themes last for the whole term while others last for half a term.

Figure 6.4   Example 2: Taking materials and components as a starting point:

Each entry in the grid shows the *introduction* of the material as a major feature of the work done. Once a material has been introduced its use will be developed in successive terms.

Outline scheme for design and technology						
YEAR	**TERM 1**		**TERM 2**		**TERM 3**	
R			Paper and card, yarn PVA glue		Reclaimed materials, Plasticine sticky tape	
1	Simple construction kits	Food (uncooked)	Plastics from reclaimed materials		Uncut wood pieces, fabrics	
2	Wood strips	More sophisticated construction kits, pulleys	Wooden dowel, wheels and axles		Food (cooked)	
3	Wire		Sheet plastic e.g. corrugated plastic		Hot glue	
4	Electrical components		Clay	Papier mâché		
5	'Plastafoam'		Balsa wood propellers			
6			Computer control components			

Alternative starting points for the scheme grid can be developed in a similar way. A grid showing the distribution of practical capability (manipulative) skills, for instance, would include:

- tearing paper;
- cutting paper;

- folding card;
- scoring card;
- cutting food products;
- making flexible joints;
- finishing fabric products;
- making pencil sketches, etc.

Moving On

In reality a co-ordinator is most likely to begin with a grid containing cross curricular topics (because, for instance, this is a requirement of a whole school approach) or specific design and technology topics or a combination of these two. From this, the design and make assignments can be developed to ensure a broad range of materials used, a progression in skills, existing successful practice and so on. Having established a framework of design and make assignments, the associated focused practical tasks (FPTs) and investigative and evaluative activities (IDEAs) can be developed.

Part of a more developed scheme might begin to look like Figure 6.5 below.

Figure 6.5 Part of an outline scheme for design and technology based on a school topic approach

YEAR		TERM 1
4	Year group topic:	The Victorians
	Design & technology topic	Toys
	Design and make assignment:	Design and make a toy for an eight-year-old child which is worked by a handle and has some moving parts.
	Focused practical tasks:	Learn how to make a variety of handles. Investigate belt and pulley systems using a construction kit.
	Evaluative activities:	Investigate some real 'Victorian' toys. Explore how any mechanisms work.
	Process skills focus:	Specifying the purpose for a product and developing criteria by which it might be evaluated.
	Materials focus:	Wooden dowel and wire
	Practical capability skills focus:	Cutting wooden dowel to length. Shaping lengths of wire using pliers. Arranging belt and pulley systems in the most effective way.
5	Year group topic D&T topic	

The development of an outline scheme will give the co-ordinator an overview for the whole school. The amount of detail will vary according to the requirements of each individual school. Additional information which might be entered on the grid or included as part of a wider document includes:

- programmes of study for the National Curriculum orders;
- broad learning objectives for each topic;
- assessment opportunities and moderation procedures;
- room availability;
- resources required for each topic;
- time available during the week/term;
- support staff available;
- references to published materials.

Eventually more detail can be recorded in a larger document which describes the full scheme for the school.

Checking the Scheme

A number of elements will have to be checked within the scheme once a basic framework has been sketched out. Checks should be made for:

- progression within all the key strands of design and technology;
- the presence of all the necessary knowledge and understanding. (Refer to National Curriculum documents and other guidelines.);
- an emphasis on all the design and make process skills. (Refer to National Curriculum documents and other guidelines.);
- a balance of materials used;
- a balance of types of design and make assignments (closed and open-ended; long and short term);
- a balance of DMAs, FPTs and IDEAs.

Progression Within the Scheme

Progression can be something which is planned for in a scheme (or individual lesson plan) or it might refer to the way in which an individual pupil proceeds in her learning. If progression through a scheme of work is well planned it will help children make their own progress. Progression is a complex issue. We know children advance in their learning at different rates and not necessarily in a linear fashion. Progress will be made more readily at certain times within some aspects of a subject than in others. It is helpful when considering the progression which might be built in to a scheme to think in terms of the strands of experience which contribute to the overall picture. The following shows how the development of an understanding of some of the various strands that make up design and technology might inter-link and progress at uneven rates.

Figure 6.6   Model to show how the strands of design and technology develop and inter-link

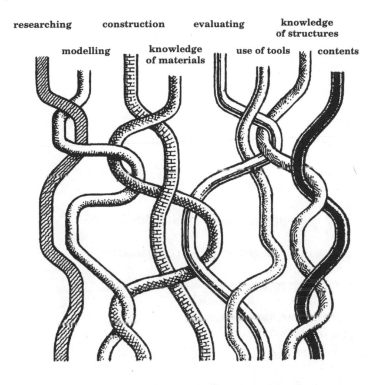

This model of strands of design and technology which overlap and evolve at different rates enables us to consider the possible progression in each strand separately.

A complete list of strands might look like this:

DESIGN PROCESS SKILLS

- Exploring and investigating skills;
- Identifying and clarifying design and make tasks;
- Specifying design criteria;
- Researching skills;
- Generating ideas;
- Modelling skills including graphic skills;
- Making skills;
- Evaluating.

KNOWLEDGE AND UNDERSTANDING STRANDS

- Understanding materials and components;
- Control involving electricity;
- Control involving mechanisms;
- Forces and structures;
- Products and applications;
- Use and knowledge of information technology.

PRACTICAL CAPABILITY STRANDS

- Materials and processes
    paper;
    card;
    reclaimed materials;
    plastics;
    wood;
    metals;
    textiles;
    clay and other mouldable materials;
    food;
    construction kits and other components;
- Use of tools;
- Construction techniques:
    marking out and measuring;
    cutting and shaping;
    joining and mixing;
    finishing.

Strands Involving Wider Issues

- Making value judgements in design and technology;
- Contexts for design and technology;
- Health and safety;
- Types of design and make tasks;
- Communicating ideas.

The processes associated with each of the materials include relevant construction techniques and the tools used. Separate strands have been included for these since a separate treatment regarding progression might be helpful. This problem of repetition, however, serves to illustrate how strands will inevitably overlap.

Each strand or group of strands can be taken and a progression mapped out across the primary school. This technique has been developed and used on teachers' courses for primary design and technology. An example of how one teacher completed the task is shown below. A simple table has been used showing each year group within the primary school. These are shown for guidance only and do not necessarily indicate exactly when a development should happen. Teachers found it helpful to complete the table for Year. R and Year. 1 first, then complete the section for Year. 6. With these two 'extremes' in mind it became easier to complete the middle sections of each table.

Figure 6.7 Planned progression in the use of clay and similar mouldable materials

	STRAND: CLAY AND OTHER MOULDABLE MATERIALS
Year	**Steps**
R	Explore Plasticine and Playdough with hands
1	Have experience of modelling with self hardening clay as well as Plasticine. Use of simple tools for texturing. Begin to understand the properties of the materials used and develop a suitable vocabulary, e.g., wet/dry; flexible/rigid; rough texture/smooth texture.
2	Introduce natural clay and begin to understand its properties. Introduce rolling and cutting techniques. Develop techniques for getting the desired texture on the clay surface.
3	Learn how to prepare clay. Introduce joining techniques – slip, pressing etc. Begin planning and designing what to make with clay, e.g., tiles.
4	Introduce thumb pots and coil pots. Introduce decoration techniques using slips and glazes. Begin to understand the firing process.
5	Emphasis on planning and designing using two and three dimensional drawings which incorporate the skills already learnt. Introduce slab pots – building, joining and decorating.
6	Carry out a project in which more than one technique might be employed. Develop confidence and control, e.g., make a relief sculpture.

This strand is concerned with a type of material and the processes that are associated with it. Other strands might be concerned with design process skills. These are often harder to map out because they deal with procedures rather than easily described skills and techniques. The following example shows how the process skill of *Specifying the requirements for a designed product* might be set out in a planned progression within a scheme.

Figure 6.8 Planned progression in specifying the requirements for a designed product

Year	Steps
STRAND: SPECIFYING THE REQUIREMENTS FOR A DESIGNED PRODUCT	
R	Pupils should be taught to: • respond to a teacher's specifications for a product they are about to design and make.
1	Pupils should be taught to: • describe the general purpose of products designed by others and respond to a teacher's specifications for a product they are about to design and make.
2	Pupils should be taught to: • add their own specifications for the product they are designing and making to those suggested by the teacher.
3	Pupils should be taught to: • devise and record a number of criteria by which the success of their own designed product can be judged.
4	Pupils should be taught to: • devise and record a wider range of criteria by which the success of their own designed product can be judged and relate these to the various ways of evaluating that product.
5	Pupils should be taught to: • clearly specify the criteria for their products with regard to a wider range of considerations such as functions and the needs of the consumer. • link their evaluations with these criteria • recognize that the method of evaluation will be influenced by the way the criteria are set out.
6	Pupils should be taught to: • devise a list of criteria for their products which take account of appearance, function, safety, reliability and the purpose for which they are intended. • suggest a variety of ways in which these criteria might be tested both subjectively and objectively.

Once a progression for a particular strand has been mapped out, it becomes a simple task to compare this with the scheme across the whole school. It is then often possible to make minor adjustments or additions to a scheme to ensure a more coherent progression within certain strands. For instance, using the example above, it would be easy to include in the scheme, an emphasis based on writing out design criteria for almost any design and make assignment carried out by a Year 3 child.

Clearly the issue of progression is a complex and time consuming one. It is one which must be worked upon over a period of years. It might help initially to choose a small number of broad strands (such as *Making Skills* or *Knowledge and Understanding*) to use as a first check in a developing scheme. Eventually, with increased experience, teachers will be able to develop their skills in greater depth in order to map a detailed progression across the curriculum.

2: Topic Plans and Lesson Plans

Planning the Details of a Design and Technology Topic

A design and technology topic might last for one lesson or a series of lessons over part or all of one term. The topic might be called a Unit of Work, a Project or by another name. The planning of individual design and technology topics will take place within the framework of a school scheme of work. The topic plan will provide the basis for the day to day lessons that make up the complete experience for each child. It often becomes the responsibility of the class teacher or group of class teachers to plan such work in consultation with the co-ordinator for design and technology.

Typically, a design and technology topic will involve one or more design and make assignments based on a common theme. Examples of such themes or contexts for design and technology are Toys and Games, Greetings Cards, The Garden or Protective Clothing. The topics for any one term will be mapped out in the scheme of work but within this constraint there will be possibilities for a wide range of suitable activities. This section describes how a class teacher might plan a suitable series of learning experiences for a group of mixed ability children.

Design and technology should not be about setting children a design task and then leaving them to get on with it, in the hope that they will learn by experience. The teacher should be involved fully in teaching a range of techniques and strategies that will improve the children's abilities in designing and making. One way of achieving this is to plan the topic in the following way.

1   CHOOSE A SUITABLE CONTEXT FOR THE TOPIC

The context for a design and technology topic will be established by considering:

- the requirements of the National Curriculum orders for design and technology;
- national guidelines for design and technology;
- the school scheme of work;
- the interests and experience of the children and their teacher;
- the resources available.

2   CONSIDER SUITABLE DESIGN BRIEFS

With a design and technology context in mind the teacher can draw up a short list of possible design and make assignments that the children might either be asked to complete or that they might choose themselves. Teachers must decide whether the children have enough experience to identify their own assignments or whether this is best provided by the teacher. Often a teacher, in discussion with the children, will have some ideas of her own which she is able to guide the children towards. An experienced teacher, however, will be ready to accept and adapt any new ideas and suggestions that the children unexpectedly provide.

Most teachers, then, will have a good idea of the kind of design and make assignments that the children will tackle within the chosen context. These tasks should:

- be relevant and of interest to the children;
- have a wide range of possible outcomes,
- have the potential for introducing the skills and knowledge the children require at that particular stage in their development;
- be manageable within the constraints of the classroom and the time available.

3   PREDICT THE DESIGN AND TECHNOLOGY OUTCOMES

At this stage in the topic planning it is a good idea to consider the kinds of outcomes for a particular assignment that might be expected of the children in the class. This involves a knowledge of the children's abilities and experience in the subject as well their likely interests and preferences.

Case Study – Making Protective Clothing

Mr Brown was planning a topic on protective clothing in which a group of Year 3 children would consider the needs of toddlers doing messy things with a paintbrush. He thought that a design and make assignment along the lines of 'Design and make some protective clothing for a 4 year old in the nursery class.' would be of interest to the group. He began to think of a variety of outcomes to the task so that he could be sure that it was suitably open-ended. He thought of aprons of various shapes and sizes, overalls and painting 'shirts'. He considered a range of materials from plastic bin liners to waterproof fabrics cut from old anoraks. He became satisfied that with the different methods for fastening the clothing as well as the design of a logo for the clothing that there would be plenty of variety in the outcomes.

4   'WORKING BACKWARDS'

Once the possible outcomes have been considered it is possible to 'work backwards' and ask the question *'In order that the children achieve the possible outcomes what skills and knowledge will they require?'* The answers to this question will enable the teacher to develop a fully structured learning programme for the whole topic which has, at its centre, the need to design and make effectively.

Case Study – Making Protective Clothing

Mr Brown considered the skills and knowledge that the children might need in order to tackle their assignment.

The children would need to know:

- *something about the problems 4-year-olds encounter when using paint;*
- *something about the protective clothing already available on the market;*
- *something about the waterproof qualities of a range of fabrics (including polythene sheet).*

The children would need to develop skills in:

- *measuring parts of the human body;*
- *making a paper pattern for an article of clothing;*
- *cutting fabrics;*
- *joining fabrics in a variety of ways;*
- *decorating fabrics;*
- *designing a logo using information technology.*

5   PLAN A STRUCTURED LEARNING PROGRAMME

Having considered the outcomes of the design and technology topic and the knowledge and skills the children need to achieve this, the teacher is then ready to plan a structured learning programme. This will consist of a combination of teacher-led activities and more open-ended pupil-led activities. In the early stages the teacher will tend to provide information and experiences for the children and this will gradually give way to a situation where the children take more and more responsibility for the path they take towards the final goal. One way of structuring a design and technology topic is shown below.

Outline of a structured learning programme for a design and technology topic

(a) Introduce the children to the context within which they will work. This may be achieved by:

- a discussion;
- reading a story or poem;
- looking at a poster, photograph or slides;
- showing a video or extracts from a CD-ROM;
- making a visit out of school;
- a survey of part or all of the school environment;
- an investigation of products designed by others;
- providing a short problem-solving activity.

(b) Identify suitable design and make assignments with the children.

(c) Discuss with the children what particular knowledge and skills they might need to carry out the assignment. Involve the children in:

- focused practical tasks which are related to the assignment;
- evaluative and investigative activities which are related to the assignment;
- other research activities related to the assignment.

(d) Ask children to consider the specifications for their designed product and to develop criteria by which its success might be judged.

(e) Provide time when the children can:

- generate ideas for their product;
- model their ideas and develop a design proposal;
- make their product;
- evaluate their product as it proceeds;
- make improvements to the product.

(f) Provide a period of time when a final reflective evaluation can be made together with a chance for children to discuss and display what they have achieved.

Providing a Purpose for the Research Activities

In this suggested programme the identification of suitable design and make assignments occurs early on. This has the advantage of providing a purpose for the introductory activities within the children's research stage. It makes a great deal of sense for children to know why they might be investigating someone else's designed product or carrying out a particular FPT. This may mean there will be a delay between the identification of the assignment and its solution but this should not be a major problem.

Case Study – Making Protective Clothing

Mr Brown's topic plan based on the outline above is as follows:

1   *Introducing the design context: Group of children visit the nursery class to 'help' with the painting corner. They are provided with a list of features to look out for.*

   •   *Discuss what they observed and the problems of keeping clothing clean.*

2   *Identification and clarification of a suitable design and make assignment that the children could carry out in the classroom. This would be something like the following:*

   •   *Design and make some full-sized protective clothing for a nursery child to be used in the painting corner in their classroom. The protective clothing should prevent paint from getting on the child's normal clothing.*

   •   *Discuss the kind of materials that can be made available and some of the techniques for construction that might be employed.*

3   *Research activities.*

   •   *Children to look at examples of protective clothing such as adult painting overalls, pinafores, dungarees, painting shirts etc. How are these fastened? Which parts of the body are protected? Are they all water proof?*

   •   *Children learn to make a paper pattern to fit the contours of the body by practising on a doll or teddy bear. They learn how to transfer this pattern to a piece of fabric by using dress making pins. (Use inexpensive polythene bags for this.)*

   •   *Children carry out an investigation into different ways of joining fabrics including polythene sheet.*

   •   *Children will measure up some of the nursery children and record their results. They might consider making a draw-around template for some of the nursery children.*

4   *Specifying the outcome: Children write out a list of five specifications for their product in a way that can be used when final evaluations are made, e.g.:*

- *The clothing should cover the front of the child including the arms and down to the knees.*

- *The clothing should be easy to get on and off for a four-year-old child.*

- *The clothing should look attractive to a four-year-old.*

5 *Children should generate ideas and model these by making a series of scale models made out of scrap paper. These can be glued on to backing paper and labelled with features such as method for fastening and the need for stitching and the material required for construction. The resulting posters will be displayed alongside the final products. The children's ability to employ this modelling strategy will be the focus for the design process skills in this topic.*

6 *Children make their protective clothing. They may need to check their progress by trying the clothing on a real nursery child every now and then.*

7 *A final evaluation can be carried out by having a fashion parade with a small number of nursery children. The designers might interview these children to gain their impressions of their new garments.*

8 *Children write a short report as a final evaluation of their project.*

Mr Brown's topic plan gives a good idea of how such a topic might be structured. It does not yet include a number of major items such as when assessment might be carried out and references to timing and resources. Individual lesson plans would need to be developed from this outline. These will include learning objectives and assessment opportunities as well as detailed resources required. These will also include references to how the work might be adapted and extended for those of differing abilities.

A format for creating a topic plan which includes all the necessary elements is included in Appendix A.

Lesson Planning

The topic plan provides the framework in which the detailed lesson plan can be developed. The lesson plan will take account of the day and time on which the activity takes place and will provide a plan for the minute by minute actions required by the teacher and the children. It should contain some clear learning objectives based on the broader ones which were developed for the topic. An example of one of Mr Brown's lesson plans is shown overleaf.

Figure 6.9   A lesson plan format for design and technology

===

Lesson Plan – Design and Technology

TOPIC: Protective clothing

Lesson focus: Modelling ideas using paper patterns

Class: 3B   **Number of children:** 28

Date: Tuesday 6 March

Time: 9.30–10.45 am

Teaching assistants:

Learning objectives:

At the end of the lesson the children should have:

- learnt how to make a paper pattern to fit an irregular shape;

- gained experience in evaluating the fit of an article of clothing.

Process skill focus:

Identifying needs	Researching	Making
Investigating the context	Generating ideas	On-going evaluation
Clarifying the task	<u>Modelling</u>	Summary evaluation
Specifying requirements	Planning and organizing	

Type of activity: DMA   <u>FPT</u>   IDEA

Resources required:

Collection of teddies or dolls (action persons etc.) classroom scissors, PVA adhesive, felt pens, plain paper.

===

Lesson outline:

	Teacher	Children
Introduction	Look at some items of clothing (shirts etc) which are not flat. Ask children to imagine what shape cloth the items are made from. Unpick a simple item and lay the fabric out flat. Establish that flat pieces of fabric are used to make clothing which fits 3D people. (Link this with work on nets in maths.)	Children on carpet listening and watching. Volunteer to hold teddy and sheet of paper.
	Show children how to find the correct shape to fit round a teddy bear by using a paper pattern which can be torn and cut by trial and error until it fits. Show how an article of clothing can be made in two halves (front and back) and then fixed together. Set children the task of making a paper set of clothes for a doll or teddy. They make a sleeveless T-shirt first then a pair of shorts.	
Development	Children work with a partner at their own desk. Once the two sides of the T-shirt have been cut and fitted these are checked by the teacher and then glued together by the children. Children go on to make a pair of shorts. Those who finish, design and make a logo for the T-shirt and glue this on. When the adhesive on the T-shirt is *dry* children try dressing the model.	Children use newspaper to 'dress' a doll or teddy. They make a sleeveless T-shirt top and pair of shorts for the doll in pairs. Children use felt pens on paper to design a logo. Children dress their doll when the glue is dry.
Conclusion	Gather children together on the carpet with any dolls which are dressed. Discuss how well various items of clothing fit. Discuss why clothing needs to fit well. Discuss how to use the paper pattern to cut a similar shape in fabric.	Children talk about how they managed the task.

Assessment:

LEARNING OBJECTIVE:

At the end of the lesson the children should have:

- learnt how to make a paper pattern to fit an irregular shape.

WHAT TO LOOK FOR:

- Ability to use trial and error to get a satisfactory fit for each paper pattern, for instance fitting and cutting the pattern more than once.

POSSIBLE QUESTIONS:

- How do you know when you have got a good fit on your teddy?
- What do you look for when you decide to cut some more paper away?

EVIDENCE GATHERED BY:

- Teacher observation and notes.
- Final product – consider how well this is cut and how well it fits.

WHICH CHILDREN:

- Blue table. (Observe more children and make notes if there is time.)

WHEN IN LESSON:

- When each child gets to the fitting stage. Approximately five minutes after children have settled at their desks.

Learning Objectives

A good lesson plan has clearly set out learning objectives. These will be based on the broad objectives that are required in the scheme and topic plan and will be related to the requirements of the National Curriculum. A learning objective in a lesson plan will describe something which most children can achieve in the lesson time. It is best set out in terms of what the children are expected to learn by the end of the lesson. For instance, examples of suitable learning objectives associated with a topic on making food packaging are:

By the end of the lesson the children should have:

- learnt about a variety of ways of protecting packaged food;
- carried out a fair test on the strength of different chocolate boxes;
- gained further experience in making 3D boxes from card nets;
- learnt three different ways of joining card when making a box;
- learnt how to score card safely;
- researched different graphic designs for the outside of a chocolate box;
- learnt how to use a computer graphics program to create a design for the lid of a box.

In some instances a whole lesson or series of lessons may address just one of these learning objectives. At other times, as in the example above, a number of objectives can be met within one lesson.

Process Skills Focus

This heading is included in the example lesson plan in order to emphasize the importance of teaching process skills. It would be easy to ignore these skills and assume that they are always being taught in any topic. An emphasis on one or two of these in any one lesson or series of lessons, however, will ensure that strategies for developing these are actually taught.

Type of Activity

Many design and technology activities will involve combinations of DMAs, FPTs and IDEAs. However, there will often be a focus on one or the other and it is helpful to be aware of this. Most FPTs and IDEAs will be teacher-led and may resemble the traditional lessons that have been found in schools for years. The DMA, at the centre of any design and technology topic, will provide a new ingredient for many teachers, requiring a different classroom organization and management.

Lesson Outline

The lesson outline can take many different forms but will generally include an introduction, development and conclusion. Teachers might like to note down their role in the lesson separately from the children's role and this is catered for in the table in this section. In this section, considerations for the special needs of certain pupils will be noted as well as any extension work for pupils who might require it.

Assessment

Assessment in any subject should be integrated with the plan for teaching that subject. The example above shows how this might be done for a design and technology lesson and is discussed in more detail in the next section.

Assessment in Design and Technology

This book has provided an analysis of what children should learn when studying design and technology in the primary school. Teachers and other interested agencies need to know just how much children have learnt at any stage by the use of effective assessment strategies.

> Assessment is the judgement teachers make about a child's attainment based on knowledge gained through techniques such as observation, questioning, marking pieces of work and testing.
>
> Dearing, 1993

It is possible to confuse teacher assessment in design and technology with the process that children use to evaluate their own work. The confusion can be avoided by asking 'What is it that is being judged?' When children evaluate their work they are making judgements about the design and make processes they have used and the products they have made. When teachers assess children's ability in design and technology they are making judgements about what has been learnt. It is a mistake to think that teachers can assess children only by judging the outcome of a design and make assignment. Furthermore, it would be wrong to assess children only by taking account of their evaluations of what they have done.

There are a number of interesting (and potentially confusing) similarities between teacher assessment and the way in which children can be encouraged to evaluate their designed products. In both cases judgements are made against criteria which may or may not have been set out beforehand and the judgements may be subjective or objective according to the criteria used.

Ritchie (1995) suggests that 'assessment can never be precise and straightforward in the way that is implied by the National Curriculum requirements . . .'. While there a great deal of truth in this, it *is* possible for teachers to increase their ability in assessing children, even when the special difficulties that a subject like design and technology provides are taken into account.

When teachers assess children's ability they do so against the learning objectives that they set out to achieve. This close link between the teacher's learning objectives and any assessments made is as important as the one between design specifications and the evaluation of the designed product. A set of clearly defined learning objectives will assist teachers in making their assessments. For instance, in the example outlined above, one learning objective was that the children should *learn how to make a paper pattern to fit an irregular shape*. The teacher's assessment was concerned with judging whether this objective had been met or not. The judgement would be made by gathering suitable evidence and making an informed decision regarding success or otherwise.

The example also shows how the teacher assessment might be planned as part of the overall lesson plan. Indeed, the assessment plan may well have an influence on the way in which the lesson is conducted. For instance if the teacher is looking for evidence of success in a particular skill then the activity must be arranged so that the child can demonstrate that skill. Also the teacher must plan to be ready to observe the particular actions of the child when these occur.

Summary of the Process of Teacher Assessment

Learning objectives	Establish clear learning objectives for a particular activity. (Based on broad learning objective set out in the scheme and topic plan.)
Activity	Plan an activity that will enable the child to demonstrate that the learning objective has been achieved.
Evidence	Decide what evidence to look for which will confirm that the objective has been achieved.
Collecting evidence	Decide how to collect the evidence and make preparations to do this. Consider suitable questions to ask.
Who	Decide *who* to assess in the time available.
When	Decide *when* to carry out the assessment.
Recording	Prepare to record the results of the assessment.

Gathering Evidence for Making Assessments in Design and Technology

Design and technology has certain characteristics which require particular assessment strategies. The practical nature of much of the subject means there is often little concrete evidence that a skill has been achieved or a particular way of thinking has occurred. Much of the learning in design and technology is to do with acquiring a practical capability and employing increasingly effective procedures. Teachers can gather evidence of success or otherwise in these areas by:

- asking searching questions at appropriate moments;
- observing actions as and when they happen;
- asking children to repeat a particular action and observing the outcome;
- listening to children's discussions;
- interpreting children's drawings and other graphic work;
- inspecting children's partly finished or completed products;
- reading or listening to children's accounts of what they intend to do or have done;
- considering children's written or oral evaluations of their own work;
- using a check list;
- giving children a controlled test in certain aspects of the subject.

The following table provides examples of learning objectives in design and technology and links these with suitable ways of gathering evidence of children's achievement.

Figure 6.10   Examples of learning objectives in design and technology

Learning objective Children should:	Evidence of achievement gathered by:	Evidence in the form of:
• learn to use a junior hacksaw to cut small sectioned wood strips safely	• teacher observation • formal test	teacher's notes test papers
• learn how to handle food products in a hygienic way	• teacher observation over an extended period of time • ticking off on a check list of aspects of hygiene • teacher questioning regarding specific hygiene rules	teacher's notes teacher's check list teacher's notes
• learn how to evaluate a product by carrying out a scientific (fair) test	• reading children's plans for such a test • observing procedure as test is carried out • questioning children regarding the variables being controlled	children's work teacher's notes teacher's notes

Learning objective Children should:	Evidence of achievement gathered by:	Evidence in the form of:
• understand the properties of corrugated plastic sheet and use this when appropriate	• look at children's labelled design drawings for evidence of appropriate use • look at children's complete or partly completed products involving corrugated plastic sheet • teacher questioning	children's drawings children's designed products teacher's notes
• learn to plan how to proceed with making a product in an organized way	• listen to children as they explain how they will proceed • read children's account of how they will proceed	teacher's notes children's written work
• understand how to make a pressure switch to control an alarm buzzer in a model	• look at finished product	children's designed products
• understand that some materials can be made into stronger components if they are folded in certain ways • understand that products designed by others have been designed with a set of purposes in mind	• observe a short problem-solving task carried out by the children • give a short oral test involving practical use of materials • give a written test using diagrams • listen to children as they discuss various aspects of designed products	teacher's notes answers recorded on teacher's question paper children's test papers teacher's notes

Assessing all the Children in a Class

Some methods for gathering evidence of children's achievement in design and technology can be used for all the children in the class in the one lesson. For instance, reading and marking children's design drawings is something that can be achieved during and after lesson time. Some forms of assessment, however, require evidence to be gathered by observation or questioning during the lesson. Teachers may not have time to observe all children within the allotted time. For instance a teacher may not be on hand to observe a modelling technique practised by each child in the class. In these instances a careful record must be kept of who has been observed and similar observations must be made for the other children during another lesson or set of lessons. For instance a teacher wanting to assess children's ability to handle food hygienically will build up a picture for each child over a series of activities and need not rely on one particular lesson.

Level Descriptions

The teacher assessment which has been described so far will provide an accumulative picture of a child's ability throughout the school year. This information will inform future topic and lesson planning as the year proceeds. The accumulated records for each child, together with the teacher's intuitive understanding of each child's ability, will also provide information for making a summative assessment using the level descriptions in the National Curriculum orders for design and technology. These are broad descriptions of what a child might be able to achieve and a 'best fit' approach is all that is required in order to allocate a level to each child. This information together with the more detailed notes a teacher will have accumulated will be reported to parents and other teachers in the school.

Summary

Design and technology is a unique subject within the primary school. There are many aspects which have been discussed in this book which need to be taught effectively by teachers if children are to become better and better at designing and making. Sound curriculum planning will enable children to become fully involved in identifying human needs and in attempting to satisfy these in increasingly effective ways.

Appendix A

TOPIC PLAN FOR DESIGN AND TECHNOLOGY

Context for topic
Topic title
Year group   Class(es)
Time available

Focus on National Curriculum programmes of study
Designing skills

Making skills

Knowledge and Understanding

Broad learning objectives

Materials focus

Cross-curricular links

Possible design and make assignments	Possible outcomes

Pupil's research
Focused practical tasks (FPTs)

Evaluative and investigative activities (IDEAs)

Learning programme
(Note down the order in which the learning events might take place)

Appendix B

Lesson plan for design and technology

LESSON PLAN – DESIGN AND TECHNOLOGY

TOPIC
Lesson focus

Class   **Number of children**
Date
Time
Teaching assistants

Learning objectives

Process skill focus

Identifying needs	Researching	Making
Investigating the context	Generating ideas	On-going evaluation
Clarifying the task	Modelling	Summary evaluation
Specifying requirements	Planning and organizing	

Type of activity   DMA   FPT   IDEA

Resources required

	Teacher	Children
Introduction		
Development		
Conclusion		

Assessment

Which children

Learning Objective

What to look for

When in lesson

Possible questions to ask

Evidence gathered by

References and Bibliography

Anning, A. (1993) 'Technological capability in primary classrooms', in J.S. Smith (ed.) *IDATER 93 The International Conference on Design and Technology Educational Research and Curriculum Development, 36–42* Loughborough: Loughborough University of Technology.

Baynes, K. (1992) *Children Designing,* Loughborough University of Technology.

Baynes, K. *et al.,* (1990) *Primary Design and Technology Guidelines,* Somerset County Council.

Bindon, A. and Cole, P. (1991) *Teaching Design and Technology in the Primary Classroom,* Blackie.

Caitlin, D. (1995) *The Inventa Book of Mechanisms,* London: Valiant Technology.

Coventry City Council Support and Advisory Service (1995) *School Development Planning in the Primary School,* Support and Advisory Service.

Cross, A. (1994) *Design and Technology 5 to 11,* London: Hodder and Stoughton.

Curriculum Council for Wales (1993) *Design and Technology – One in Five,* CCW.

Danby, M. (ed.) (1989) *Working with Teachers,* Coventry: National Council For Educational Technology (NCET).

Dearing, R. (1994) *The National Curriculum and its Assessment,* London: School Curriculum and Assessment Authority.

Department for Education (1995) *Key Stages 1 and 2 of the National Curriculum,* London: HMSO.

Department for Education and Employment (1996) *Looking at Values Through Products and Applications (Conference proceedings),* London: DfEE.

Department of Education and Science (1987) *Craft, Design and Technology from 5 to 16,* London: HMSO.

Department of Education and Science and the Welsh Office (1988) *Science for ages 5–16 – Proposals of the Secretary of State,* London: HMSO.

Department of Education and Science and the Welsh Office (1990) *Technology in the National Curriculum,* London: HMSO.

Design and Technology Association (1995a) *Guidance Materials for Design and Technology – Key Stages 1 and 2,* Wellesbourne: DATA.

Design and Technology Association (1995b) *Technical Vocabulary for Key Stages 1 and 2,* Wellesbourne: DATA.

Design and Technology Association (1996) *The Design and Technology Primary Co-ordinators' File,* Wellesbourne: DATA.

Design Council Primary Education Working Party (1987) *Design and Primary Education.* London: The Design Council.

Durbin, G. *et al.,* (1990) *A Teacher's Guide to Learning from Objects,* London: English Heritage.

Engineering Council, Standing Conference on Schools Science and Technology (SCSST) (1985) *Problem Solving: Science and Technology in Primary Schools,* London: Engineering Council.

Gunnell, B. *et al.,* (1991) *One Step at a Time – A Journey Beneath the Key Stages 1 and 2 Programmes of Study for Design and Technology,* Gloucestershire: Gloucestershire County Council.

Hennessy, S. and McCormick, R. (1994) *The General Problem Solving Process in Technology Education – Myth or Reality?* in F. Banks *Teaching Technology,* London: Routledge.

Idle, I. K. (1991) *Hands-on Technology,* Cheltenham: Stanley Thornes.

Johnsey, R. (1994) 'How to Control Movement', The Big Paper, 25, 8–9.

Johnsey, R. (1995a) An Analysis of the Procedures used by Primary School Children as they Design and Make, MSc thesis, Warwick University.

Johnsey, R. (1995b) 'The place of the process skill making in design and technology, lessons from research into the way primary children design and make' in J. S. Smith (ed.) *IDATER 05 The International Conference on Design and Technology Educational Research and Curriculum Development, 15–20* Loughborough: Loughborough University of Technology.

Johnsey, R. (1995c) 'The design process – Does it exist? – A Critical Review of Published Models for the Design Process in England and Wales', *The International Journal of Technology and Design Education.* 2.

Johnsey, R. (1995d) 'Criteria for Success', *Design and Technology Teaching,* 27, 2, 37–39.

Johnson, P. (1992) *Pop-up Paper Engineering,* London: Falmer Press.

Kelly, A. V. *et al.,* (1987) *Design and Technological Activity – A Framework for Assessment,* London: Assessment of Performance Unit/HMSO.

Kimbell, R. *et al.,* (1991) *The Assessment of Performance in Design and Technology,* London: APU/SEAC.

Mayo, S. (1993) 'Myth in Design', *International Journal of Design Education,* 3, 1, 41–52.

National Association of Advisers and Inspectors in Design and Technology. *Make It Safe!,* NAAIDT.

National Council for Educational Technology, (1989) *Primary Technology – The Place of Computer Control,* Coventry: NCET.

National Curriculum Council (1992) *National Curriculum Technology: The Case for Revising the Order,* York: NCC.

National Curriculum Council (1993a) *Knowledge and Understanding of Science – Electricity and Magnetism, A Guide for Teachers,* York: NCC.

National Curriculum Council (1993b) *Knowledge and Understanding of Science – Forces, A Guide for Teachers,* York, NCC.

Naughton, J. (1994) *What is Technology?* in Banks, F. (ed.) *Teaching Technology,* London: Routledge.

Outterside, Y. R. (1993) *The Emergence of Design Ability: The Early Years* in J.J. Smith (ed.) IDATER 93, Loughborough: Loughborough University of Technology.

Ritchie, R. (1995) *Primary Design and Technology – A Process for Learning,* London: Fulton.

Rowlands, D. and Holland, C. (1989) *Problem Solving in Primary Science and Technology.* Cheltenham: Stanley Thornes.

School Curriculum and Assessment Authority (1995a) *Key Stages 1 and 2 Design and Technology – The New Requirements,* London: SCAA..

School Curriculum and Assessment Authority (1995b) *Key Stages 1 and 2 Information Technology – The New Requirements,* London: SCAA.

School Examinations and Assessment Council (1991) *INSET Materials for Key Stage 1 Standard Assessment Tasks,* SEAC.

Williams, P. and Jinks, D. (1985) *Design and Technology 5–12,* London: Falmer Press.

Index

Index

Titles in the Children, Teachers and Learning series:

Children, Teachers and Learning Series

General Editor: Cedric Cullingford

Exploring Primary Design and Technology